SCHOOLED BY THE SMOKIES

Life Lessons Learned on the Trail

by Dan Nobles,
a.k.a. Wandering Monk

 TRILOGY

Schooled by the Smokies: Life Lessons Learned on the Trail

Trilogy Christian Publishers A Wholly Owned Subsidary of Trinity Broadcasting Network

2442 Michelle Drive Tustin, CA 92780

Cover design by: Natalee Dunning

For information about special discounts for bulk purchases, please contact Trilogy Christian Publishing.

Trilogy Disclaimer: The views and content expressed in this book are those of the author and may not necessarily reflect the views and doctrine of Trilogy Christian Publishing or the Trinity Broadcasting Network.

Manufactured in the United States of America

10 9 8 7 6 5 4 3 2 1

Library of Congress Cataloging-in-Publication Data is available.

ISBN: 978-1-68556-603-6

E-ISBN: 978-1-68556-604-3

Special thanks to:
Connie, my wife, who supports my wandering even when she doesn't understand why I like sleeping in a tent.
My daughters, who inspire me by their own dreams.
My grandkids, who give me a reason to share my stories and who I hope will share their stories one day.

This is dedicated to
the Creator who blessed us with the beauty of creation.

TABLE OF CONTENTS

Class, Let the Adventures Begin!

"The mountains are calling and I must go."
—John Muir

Hi, y'all, Dan here. Thanks for joining me. I've used that greeting to open each of my videos. It just seems right to begin this book with the same familiar words. It's sort of a tradition of mine. As I adventured these old paths, they began to teach me lessons on life as well as how to negotiate the challenge of their trails. Join me as I explore ten maxims that resonated with my companions in the Smokies. Together, let's be schooled by the Smokies.

Hikers have many customs and traditions. One tradition is the trail name. My trail name is Monk. I guess "Monk" is my trail surname. That makes "Wandering" be my trail first name. Although my legally given name is Dan, the hiking community knows me as Wandering Monk. That may seem odd to some, but hikers get their identity from the trail. They may do something, say something, or just find themselves somewhere, and that may earn the much-desired trail name. Other hikers give us our name.

We can accept it or not, but eventually, we will become known by our trail name. It's just one of many customs that endear us to one another and to the trail. It's one of the traditions that shape us.

The stories and experiences that I share describe lessons the trail has taught me along the miles. Hiking is a whole person experience of the body, mind, and spirit. As we share the adventures of various trails, I hope that you begin to sense something bigger than yourself is waiting and inviting you to come and be awed by its beauty. There is an old German word that expresses the echoes that draw us to experience nature in its fullness. The word is *fernweh* and transliterates as "far sick." It suggests a homesickness for that place where I have never been before. It is like a shadow or an echo of a voice that I have never heard but sounds so very familiar that I yearn to hear it again. *Fernweh* draws me to the trail, and it motivates me to keep returning to it.

I believe there is a seed of *fernweh* in each of us. There is something that keeps pulling us forward. *Fernweh* motivated explorers to sail across oceans and discover new lands that were unknown. It drove settlers from comfortable homes in the east to carve out new lives in the great prairies of Kansas, Nebraska, and Oklahoma. It burned in the souls of families who tackled the wilds of the Oregon Trail until that ran into the Pacific coast. It is the flame that drives exploration in every field of study to find new discoveries. It pushes us to hike old paths in ancient ways.

The trail teaches each of us as we open ourselves to her. She makes us vulnerable by challenging us physically, mentally, and spiritually. One good friend and fellow hiker shared her insights. Darlene McGarrity permitted me to share her words. She wrote:

The Appalachian Trail will highlight your biggest fears and accent your greatest weakness. Your character defects will glare like water in the sun. "Know thyself" will become a mantra as you tackle a journey unlike any other. Ideas like "false self" and "true self" take on a new meaning as you ask yourself every day, "Why am I here?" A dozen different answers will swirl in your head like the ice cream you've been dreaming about for four days. You'll meet and engage with people that you wouldn't bat an eyelash at on the street. You will connect with many of them. Others will remind you of the very demons you wish to shed. Know thyself. You'll become who you always were…the layers of societal norms will be stripped away. You'll be left with yourself in such rawness you won't recognize the pettiness you once complained about. That's just in the first 300 miles.

Darlene's powerful insight is true. When we slow down from our fast-paced lives where we are flying down the interstate, across oceans, or through the sky, we discover many things that are often overlooked. When we slow down to hike at one or two miles per hour, we find God's speed. We begin to see that flowers and trees are individual things and not merely fields and forests. We see squirrels, birds, deer, bears, elk, snakes, worms, caterpillars, and all types of critters. The complexities of life's busyness are eclipsed by the simple as we slow our pace enough to see the trail.

The simplicity of hiking may be the tap root from which all other lessons grow. The lesson of simplicity that I learned has two parts. First, simple is seldom the same thing as easy. Simplicity is often dismissed as something that is quick and easy. However, such thinking is flawed, and the value of the simple is lost because we desire to be sophisticated and wise. As we collect letters after our name, we become too intelligent to waste time considering the simple. We seek to unravel the complexities of life. However, we are poorer for overlooking the simple. No, simple is not the same as easy. In fact, simply walking step by step, climbing up 3,000 feet to reach the summit of a mountain is much more challenging than driving along winding roads through Colorado propelled by a powerful engine in the luxury of a car. Cars are complex machines, and roadways are engineering marvels, but walking along worn paths brings an entirely different reality to the simplicity of nature. Simple is seldom easy.

Another fundamental lesson of simplicity is that when it's given sufficient time, the simple often reveals us to ourselves. Academia is infatuated with formulating complex theories and ideas. When issues arise, we create elaborate descriptions, provocative labels, and unproven solutions to address the problem. If there is no problem, we will even create one so that we can develop a solution for it. Why are we so attracted to the complex? Perhaps it is because we can hide ourselves from ourselves in the complexities of our self-made issues. We can shift the spotlight from our own weaknesses, flaws, and imperfections by highlighting the weaknesses, flaws, and imperfections of societies, systems, and, well…others. If I can spotlight your issues, then I can ignore my own.

We can't hide in the simple. There isn't enough cover to slip behind so that you don't see my stuff. More disturbing, though, I can't hide from myself in the simple. While in the complex, I can hide, but also the beauties of life are hidden as well. There are hard lessons filled with great joy in the simple things.

I recall hiking in the Smoky Mountains. One morning, after a cold and rainy night, one of my fellow hikers said, "Let's plan to stay in a shelter tonight." The thought was so encouraging and exciting that I was motivated all day by the simple idea of sleeping in a ready-made shelter and not setting up my tent. Evening came, and the shelter was full. I had to pitch my tent after all, but it really didn't matter. Rather than being disappointed, I realized that my entire day had been made better by the simple thought of possibly staying in a shelter.

The trail has so many great lessons to teach. If I only open myself to learn, she will freely share her wisdom. So I hope that I am able to share some of her lessons with you in the following pages. I hope that she forgives my limited abilities and that you are able to fill in the gaps with your experiences. Just remember to keep it simple and *stay on the path!*

CHAPTER 1
FOR EVERY DOWN, THERE'S AN UP

"Somewhere between the bottom of the climb and the summit is the answer to the mystery why we climb."
—Greg Child

Someone added up all the elevations along the Appalachian Trail and discovered that hiking the nearly 2,200 miles from Georgia to Maine is equivalent to climbing Mount Everest sixteen times! After hiking through northern Georgia, I thought that I had already accomplished that goal already, if not a few more mountains too.

The climbs and descents are constant on the trail. Flat, smooth paths were rare treats, and I quickly realized the impact to my walking speed. While I could comfortably walk three miles in an hour on local trails, the Appalachian Trail demanded about an hour of walking to complete one mile. So, after a full day of climbing to the peaks of mountains and descending into gaps, I had covered about eight miles. Perhaps that is why the shelters in Georgia were constructed at eight-mile intervals. This reality taught me a lesson about listening to those who have gone before me, but that is a different maxim for a later chapter.

The trail introduces herself quickly. Desiring to squeeze every experience from every opportunity, I wanted to hike the Approach Trail to the top of Springer Mountain. Springer is the official beginning for hikers who trek north toward Maine. The approach trail is about eight and a half miles that lead up from the base of Amicalola Falls to the top of Springer. *Amicalola* is a Cherokee word meaning "tumbling waters." At 729 feet tall, that beautiful waterfall is the third highest cascading waterfall east of the Mississippi River. There are two sets of stairs to get to the top. The first set of stairs includes 175 steps. The sign at the beginning states, "Difficulty: Strenuous," and that is the general description of the following 2,193.1 miles of the Appalachian Trail.

As I climb that staircase, the beautiful sights and sounds of the waterfalls are ever before me. At their invitation, the first climb wasn't as difficult as I anticipated. However, after walking across a short bridgeway, there stood a second staircase. Here the sign warned, "West Ridge Staircase. Difficulty: Strenuous. 425 Steps. Top of Falls. Lodge. AT Approach." Now things got interesting! After 600 steps, I got to start climbing the approach to Springer Mountain.

The first day was filled with ascending the path that culminated in an underwhelming summit of Springer Mountain.

There were a few rocks at the top of Springer and a small view of the surrounding mountains and valleys. A hole about the size of a car's glove compartment had been hewn into the side of one rock, and a logbook was kept behind a metal door guarding that space. Hikers sign the logbook to document their point of entry into their adventure.

Climbing up mountains became a daily exercise. Those climbs tested my legs and back as I carried my thirty-pound pack. In that pack was everything that I needed to survive on the trail. Its contents included my tent, sleeping bag, clothes, repair kit to fix any potential gear failures, and a first aid kit to fix any potential body failures, as well as my food for the days ahead.

The climbs tested my legs, but my lungs were my greatest limiting factor physically. I thought that I had prepared, but I quickly learned that I was wrong. I would find myself sucking air and trying to garner the strength to keep going. Just when I wasn't sure that I could go farther, a young man (his trail name was Big Spoon) came by and sat down with me. He was tired too, which soothed my bruised ego and made me feel a little better. He casually said, "This ain't no race." Those few words gave me the inspiration that I needed to tackle the hills ahead. His voice echoed in my memory each time I would start a climb, "This ain't no race." I would smile, slow my pace, and steadily ascend the rise. Soon, I was standing at the top and thinking that this one was easier than the last. My body gained strength from the climbs.

Sometimes the climbs and descents were mundane, with no views beyond the treacherous roots and rocks that seemed to jump from the ground to trip me up. Hikers refer to those areas as *PUDs*, which means *Pointless Ups and Downs*. I tried to constantly remember a comment by another hiker. His trail name was Wild on the Trail, and I had watched his videos last year. Wild often said, "You're always one step from going home." He warned that hikers must be careful to watch where they walked to prevent tripping and injuring themselves. I tried to keep that in mind, especially going downhill and especially going downhill in the rain over slick rocks. There seemed to be a lot of PUDs somedays.

Other climbs and descents were nearly magical. I enjoyed waking early, taking down my tent, filling my backpack, turning on my headlamp, and getting on the trail before sunrise. I enjoyed the darkness of the trail, illuminated only by the light beam that extended coming from the little lamp held by an elastic band around my head. The quietness of the trail was soothing. The inability to see the path ascending the mountainside helped take away the sinking feeling I always had whenever I focused on the obstacle ahead. Then, slowly at first, the birds began to sing their wake-up songs. There were the rustling sounds of critters scampering around in the darkness. Could they see better than me? The sun began to hint that it was coming. The skies began to glow with beautiful colors that would not be seen again until the following morning at the same time. There were hints of purples and blues that turned into pinks, yellows, and reds. Then the fiery sun broke upward and grew to chase away the remaining darkness. As its rays filtered through the trees, light reflected the tree trunks, and their bark looked like smoldering coals. I had to look closely to be sure they were not burning for real. Such scenes taught me that the ups and downs were not pointless after all. They all had meaning that waited to be shared with me if I would slow down long enough to be taught by the trail.

Sometimes I thought that I was forever climbing, and eventually, I would step through the atmosphere, through the cosmos, and into heaven itself. However, that wasn't true. I wasn't always climbing up. For every up, there was a down. In the beginning, I treasured the downs. I remember my brother Rick telling me, "We have to speed up on the downs and flat areas to make up for time lost on the ups." Well, Rick, that is a nice thought, but it has two major flaws. First, there were no flat spots! And second, the downs were as hard as the ups!

There are probably a few flat spots on the Appalachian Trail, but I just haven't found them yet. Still, the downs were treacherous! The ups challenged my lungs, and the downs destroyed my old knees.

Blood Mountain is one of those iconic and infamously notorious challenges in the early part of the northbound trek of the trail. The tallest mountain in Georgia, Blood Mountain, stands 4,442 feet tall, and one climbs about 650 feet in a mile. This was the first big climb, but there were many others that were bigger. Still, the reputation of Blood Mountain was as intimidating as its name for hikers who were getting started on the trail. Personally, I didn't find Blood Mountain as hard as I had anticipated. It gave me several great gifts that I am very thankful for even now. It was a huge confidence boost. A major milestone was completed, and I survived! I learned to take breaks on the climb. There are some natural points up the mountain where the path isn't as steep as others. Those points became my rest spots. I would climb a mile, stop and take off my backpack, and rest for a good break. Remembering my brother on previous hikes, asking, "Is this a one or two Snickers climb?" I would eat some candy for quick energy and start up the mountain again. Soon I was at the top, and the view was amazing!

The view from the peak of Blood Mountain was a great reward for the effort to get there. That was a huge gift. The second gift was meeting and getting to know Mike. Mike was a fellow veteran who retired from the US Navy (I'm retired army). We began to talk and develop a friendship there on the top of Blood Mountain. Mike had previously had both of his knees replaced, and downs were challenging for him. So, for the next several days, we hiked together. He was faster on the ups than me, and I would catch up and pass him on the downs. We averaged about the same speed overall. Mike was easy to talk with, and we got along better than anyone else that I've met on the trail. We both decided to stay on top of the mountain that night. A boy scout troop arrived and camped there as well. It was a great evening.

The following morning, I awoke to an amazing sunrise. The clouds had settled in the valley and looked like soft cotton waves in an ocean. The surrounding mountain peaks looked like islands peeking through the cloudy ocean. The sun was bright, and its rays reflected shadows from the peaks across the tops of the clouds. I stood there mesmerized by the view. Several of the scouts were standing around me. I told them that this was a Psalm 121 (ESV) moment. They looked puzzled, and I told them to look it up and read it aloud, "I lift up my eyes to the hills. From where does my help come? My help comes from the LORD, who made heaven and earth. He will not let your foot be moved…" I would need some of that strength to descend the backside of Blood Mountain.

Coming down Blood Mountain was terrible! The descent off the mountain was much harder than the ascent had been. There were slick rock faces where I sat and slid down to the boulders below. On the boulders, I had to pick and choose where to step, where to hold with my hands, or where to place my trekking poles so that

I didn't fall perilously to my early death. That's an exaggeration, of course; I never felt that I would die, but I wondered how the rescue teams would carry out my broken body. The point is that downs can be just as challenging as ups. That lesson has remained true for every trail and on every hike that I have experienced.

Another challenging descent was going into Unicoi Gap. Mike and I had stayed at the Low Gap Shelter area. I set up my tent and fell asleep, very satisfied with the solitude of my little home. The trail was beginning to get crowded. It would swell much more through the Smoky Mountains that lay ahead. There was a threat of rain for the evening and the next day. Several were staying in the shelter to keep their gear dry. The incoming weather front cooled the trail. Those who stayed in the shelter put a tarp up over its open eastern entrance to block the cold wind. The rains came, and the next morning, I struck camp in between showers. As was my preferred habit, I started down the trail in the dark, but that morning I had the added company of cold rain.

The path quickly filled with water, and I splashed up the trail out of Low Gap, laughing to myself about fording the Appalachian Stream while moving toward my next destination of the day. The afternoon was filled with a steady descent down into Unicoi Gap. The rocks and roots that I had become accustomed to on the path were now slick from the rain. Some were hidden under the stream that had been converted from the path. Wild's warning resounded in my head, "You are always one step away from going home." I crept slowly down to a large wooden sign announcing my arrival to Unicoi Gap. Mike and I called a shuttle, and soon we were drying out at Your Home in the Woods Hostel. Paul and Bonnie, who have owned this place for twenty-seven years, were the perfect hosts. The hot shower was much needed and deeply appreciated. It was only seconded by the wonderful dinner.

Mike and I were now warm and dry. We were excited for the adventures ahead for the moment. Then my plans changed with a phone call from home. Just like the physical downs on the trail, emotional downs are inevitable. My wife, Connie, called, and her voice revealed her own valley. Her sister was very sick, and Connie was compelled to go to Kansas to help with her sister's care. I could have been misreading the tone of her voice, but after forty-four years of marriage, we begin to sense one another's emotions and needs. Connie needed me to go with her. Still, she didn't want to interrupt my dream of this adventure. She wouldn't ask me to go with her. I was truthful when I told her that I was willing and wanted to go with her. There is a huge difference between dreams and needs. I had been working on being mentally flexible enough to recognize and prioritize those differences so that I might choose the greater path. The trail was teaching me to slow down, and I knew that it would still be here, waiting for my return.

The next morning, Connie picked me up from the hostel, and it was a very sweet moment. It was hard to say goodbye to Mike. He had become a good friend. Friendships form quickly when people share a common challenge to achieve a common goal. However, it was wonderful to see Connie. We had also endured many years of common challenges. Bonnie and Paul had also become friends. Paul and I had several short conversations but always wanted more time to share our stories. Bonnie has a servant's heart and is very kind. She wanted to pray for us. So, before we drove away, we held hands and prayed for protection, health, and reunions. The emotional descent was filled with rocks and roots to trip the heart.

We were needed in Kansas, especially Connie, and we worked together to arrange medical care. Connie helped her sister to be as comfortable as possible and encouraged everyone. Her sister lives on large wheat and cattle farm outside the little town of Mound Valley in southeast Kansas, population 407. Connie and I laughingly call it the vortex. The only cell phone signal we could get was standing beneath a large tree on the corner of her sister's property, and that was spotty at best. If I held my phone just right and turned to the south, then I could get a signal—sometimes. Otherwise, I had to drive to the big city of Mound Valley and sit outside the library (yes, there is a small library in a little building shared with the town hall). There was Wi-Fi there that allowed us to send virtual smoke signals to communicate with the outside world.

Our inability to surf the net was certainly a first-world problem, but at that time, it really was a problem. We needed to research the medical care industry. The little local hospital was failing Connie's sister. Their attitude was more about what they couldn't (or wouldn't do) than trying to determine what they could do. After several meetings with the administration and doctors, we began to make some progress. We were in a rocky and challenging gap, but for every down, there is an up.

After a week of support, Connie's sister was feeling a little stronger. We wondered if she wanted us to go more than she was really improving. Perhaps she felt like a burden and simply wanted us to go home. Anyway, we thought that arrangements were coming together for her care. We also needed to attend to things back home that had been placed on hold while we were in Kansas. And the trail was calling for me back. So we drove the thousand miles to North Carolina. It was a good trip. Connie and I enjoyed the time together to reflect and laugh. We were ascending those paths of the soul, and we felt stronger as we climbed.

Interruptions provide opportunities for reassessing plans. I decided to jump ahead from where I got off the trail in order to get back on my time schedule. Instead of returning to Unicoi Gap, I was picked up by a friend who wanted to hike a section with me. We went to the Nantahala Outdoor Center in North Carolina and started north from there. Of course, that meant that I would return to the NOC and hike the 87 miles south to Unicoi Gap after summiting Katahdin in Maine. At least, those were my thoughts at the time.

My friend David wanted to hike with me through a portion of the Smoky Mountains. There are challenges when someone wants to hike along. Challenges that neither of us had considered. An obvious challenge is the differences in goals. David thought of the trail in terms of a few days. He thought we could hike from the NOC to Newfound Gap in five days. Had that been the final destination, we might have pushed hard and into the night to accomplish his goal. However, my eyes were focused on a much longer goal. If I was going to hike another 2,100 miles, I would have to pace myself in order to conserve energy and avoid injury. The ups and downs demand a price on my body. I wasn't willing to pay that price in one relatively short section. This was a big difference in our goals that we had not discussed.

Another challenge was our different physical limitations. I have already shared my preference of waking up early each morning. Getting up by 5 a.m. and stepping onto the trail before sunrise is rewarding to me. However, I don't like to hike late in the evenings. By 5 p.m., my body is tired; my legs are weak, and I am ready to stop for the evening. That's a twelve-hour day, and my entire being cries out, "Enough!" and it's time to stop. David's rhythm is much different. Due to a heat injury from years past, he doesn't sleep well. So he stays awake until early morning and sleeps until late morning. By the time he was finally ready to hike, I was frustrated with the thought that we only had five or six hours to hike. David was thinking we could still do twelve to fifteen miles. I was thinking, *I haven't done fifteen miles in a day on the entire journey. What makes you think we can do it in half a day?* The ups of getting back on the trail were clashing with the downs of unmet expectations—for both of us.

Still, we did enjoy the comradery and the spectacular views from the mountain vistas. We endured the ascents coming up from the NOC, climbing Jacob's Ladder, and hiking through the ridges of the Appalachians in southern North Carolina. We took a NERO at the Hiker's Inn, where Tom and Nancy were our hosts. During that NERO, David decided that he would stop at Fontana Dam and not go into the Smokies. He realized that we were slower (at least I was slower) than he had planned, and he would need to return home to teach his class at UNC School of the Arts.

Early the following morning, I wrote a note to say bye to David as he slept. Tom, the motel owner, drove me back to the Yellow Creek parking lot, and I resumed my hike by climbing out of the gap. I was ascending once again, physically and emotionally. While I regretted that David hadn't fulfilled his goal, I was happy to be hiking alone and following my own rhythm of the trail. I wanted to really embrace the saying, "Hike your own hike."

There is great satisfaction when the physical and emotional rhythms of the trail are in synch. It seems to me that I feel light; my steps are smoother; the path is less jarring to my old joints, and everything is more enjoyable. There is a lesson to be learned in embracing the trail and choosing to have an attitude of joy. It sounds simple, but simple is seldom easy.

As I hiked toward Fontana, I met several other hikers. One was a man that I had met on my first day at the Amicalola Falls Lodge on the day I began this adventure. Barney, now his trail name was "Rerun," was sitting in a shelter cooking lunch. There were a couple of other men there, Craig (who had no trail name yet) and Gourmet (I never learned his real-world name). They were all thru-hikers who planned to walk the entire length of the Appalachian Trail over the next five or six months. We laughed together and shared stories of our adventure thus far. I felt better that Rerun was here. Maybe my time off the trail had not delayed my hike too much after all. Of course, there was the section that I had skipped to get to this point, but I would catch up with that later. For now, the Smokies loomed large before me.

My plan was to hike to the Fontana "Hilton" Shelter, spend the night, and enter the Smoky Mountains on the next day. Craig invited me to join the others for a steak dinner in Fontana Village. A dinner and a bed before the Smokies proved to be too much temptation to pass, so we hiked down the mountain toward Fontana Village. On the way, I saw my first glimpse of the sprawling lake down in the valley. The blue body of water was camouflaged by the leafless trees that skirted the trail. Its subtleness was beautiful. The beauty grew as I descended the mountain path. Suddenly the beauties of God's creation framed the beauties of human construction. There was an opening in the trees, and the massive Fontana Dam stood before me. Standing fifty stories tall, it is the largest concrete dam east of the Rocky Mountains.

After an evening of good food and visiting with my new friends, I spent much of the night editing and uploading videos to share with my YouTube audience. I enjoy making those videos. They offer an opportunity to reflect on the day, and I can respond to those reflections by editing and sharing the story. All seemed right with my hike.

Ox, a great person and one of the super trail maintainers of the Appalachian Trail, was standing in the lobby of the Fontana Inn as I checked out. He offered me a ride to the trailhead and delivered me there with a ton of great advice and stories of his own experiences. Soon, I was back on the trail crossing Fontana Dam and immediately ascending the big climb into the Great Smoky Mountains National Park. It was intimidating to enter this mountain chain and its reputation of being a grueling task.

The first climb was just as hard as I had imagined. For me, it was the hardest climb that I had encountered on the Appalachian Trail. Blood Mountain and Jacob's Ladder paled beside this obstacle. Between the beginning of the climb and the Shuckstack Fire Tower that stood on top of this peak, there was a grueling 3,000-foot ascent over a three-mile trek. There were no switchbacks and no flat spots. Only a continuous, monotonous, seemingly endless climb. My emotional desire and physical strength were diametrically opposed. It wasn't good. I remember thinking, *Maybe I am too old for this, too out of shape, not good enough to do it. Maybe this is the end of my journey.* Just then, a young man named John came along. He simply said, "This is the hardest one yet." That was all it took. I realized that this young man was struggling with the same physical challenge that I was facing. I wasn't alone in my pain. I told him that he had inspired me to get to the top. I think my words surprised and encouraged him too.

Sometimes we don't really need wise advice. The simplest, unassuming words shared in compassion and sincerity are often the most powerful motivation we need to push forward. There is great power in knowing that someone just recognizes and understands. Mike had given me a shot in the arm to make it to the top of that climb. We arrived at the top and found several others there. They had succeeded in dragging themselves there too. Everyone was sitting around a small stream, collecting water in bottles, bags, and other containers. They squeezed water from one container, through various filters, and into their bottles. Some were drinking heavily from their filtered water, and others were hoarding their newly filled bottles like precious treasures for the journey. Then a young woman—her trail name is Rose—told me, "Monk, you really need to go up the tower."

There is a fire tower about a quarter mile off the trail at the peak of Shuckstack. The tower offered a 360-degree panoramic view of the lower Smoky Mountains. The day was clear, and the views would be beautiful, but my legs were burning, and I didn't want to waste any energy climbing yet higher on this mountain. Still, Rose encouraged me, saying, "It's an easy path, and you'll regret it if you don't go." She had lied! It wasn't an easy path. The path was filled with rocks and boulders. It was more climbing. I shouted, "I hate you, Rose!" I heard her laughter echo through the trees and up the path.

When I finally made it to the tower, the view was beautiful beyond description. I climbed the full height of the tower and just stood there. I was mesmerized by the sight. I owed Rose much gratitude for pushing me on. She stands in line with many others to whom I am so grateful for little words, smiles, or nods that came at just the right time to raise me to heights that I would have missed if they had not been there. We depend on one another to reset us to where the physical and emotional ups and downs collide, and our words help us to appreciate life as it unfolds before us.

The rest of the day, my body and my soul felt lighter, more energized, and ready for the challenges that lay ahead. I stopped at the only tent site in the Smoky Mountains along the Appalachian Trail. The site sat down in a low spot—in the South, we call it a holler—and it was filled with tents. I had run face-first into the bubble! The bubble is another hiking term for a large crowd of hikers who are not necessarily intending to walk together but come together like cars in a traffic jam at a busy intersection in rush hour. There were probably twenty-five tents scattered around this place. Fortunately, the young man who had encouraged me earlier and I had spotted a small, flat space just off the trail before the path leading down to the main tent site. We decided to pitch our tents up there for the night.

In the night, I began to panic, "How will I be able to find the solitude I crave in the middle of all these people?" Again, at just at the right time, Connie sent a text message about folks going out on the Oregon Trail to start lives out west. She wrote, "…people traveling west and encountering obstacles and often not even knowing if they are headed in the right direction. They endured much and persevered. You will too." Her words and the blessings embedded in that message were like strong, prevailing winds that filled the sails of my soul. I knew that wherever the path took me, I would be a grateful participant. The trail and I were friends on this journey. She would be a great teacher, and I wanted to learn from her.

The ups and downs continued through the Smokies. They soaked into every aspect of the experience, often literally soaking in through the spring rains. There was a series of days where the sun filled and warmed the trail, but the next day was raining and cold. I guess that's March in the mountains. I was beginning to get into the rhythm of grueling ascents followed by treacherous descents. The climb to the top of Clingmans Dome was surprisingly survivable. The Dome is the tallest peak on the Appalachian Trail. It towers above the surrounding mountains at 6,612 feet.

The hike up the path to Clingmans Dome was wonderful. As the elevation increased, the vegetation began to change. Spruces replaced pines, and fluorescent green moss covered everything. The sun's rays pierced through the trees and onto the trail, creating a beautiful and mystical light show. I thought a gnome or leprechaun might jump from behind a fallen tree and demand toll for passage. It was the most beautiful five miles that I had seen since leaving Amicalola Falls, and there had been many beautiful scenes. These beauties played with my imagination and distracted me from focusing on my oxygen-deprived lungs. Soon, I reached the top of Clingmans Dome. The day was bright and clear and amazing. My emotional high was in harmony with this physical ascent. Everything seemed right, and it was glorious!

Rick, my brother who got me into this crazy hobby of backpacking, drove from Alabama to pick me up at Clingmans. He brought me an awesome trail magic. Trail magic is an unexpected treat that folks give to hikers along the trail. It comes in various forms. Trail magic is often food or drinks but sometimes rides to do laundry or even lodging to rest in the comforts of a real bed and maybe even a shower. Those who give trail magic are known as "Trail Angels," and they are loved by hikers! Rick must be an archangel of the trail. He gave me everything; food, laundry, food, shower, food, hotel to sleep, and did I mention—*food*! It was a great treat. I always enjoy the opportunity to visit with Rick, but this was special.

For every down, there's an up, and for every up, there is a down. The down came quickly after a restful and rewarding stay with my brother. We drove back to the Clingmans Dome parking lot in the cold rain. Walking up the long, paved path that leads to the trailhead, I was quickly reminded that the weather report forecasted a full day of rain and wind. The good news was that I was going downhill. So, once I climbed up to the trailhead, then I began the descent toward Newfound Gap. As usual, the descent was filled with rocks and roots sticking up from the ground to trip me. Coupled with the streams of water that cascaded around and over my feet, it was another slippery challenge. It was actually fun, as I embraced the trail for what she offered that day.

The down continued as I descended into the parking lot at Newfound Gap. This popular point draws many visitors traveling from Gatlinburg, Tennessee, to wherever they are going next. Even in the cold wind and rain, it was filled with cars and people today. I wanted to stop at a sign where you can have one foot in Tennessee and one foot in North Carolina. Connie and I had been there years before after our daughter's wedding in Pigeon Forge. We had even walked up the trail a bit and laughed about crazy people who hiked up that steep, winding, rocky path. Now, here I stood. The crowds were lined up to get their pictures taken standing in two states at once. It was too much for me, and I decided to move on.

Just as I was walking away to get started on the trail, a young man asked if I was a hiker. I looked down at my wet pants and my soaked raincoat, adjusted my backpack, and said, "Yes, I am. How did you know?" We laughed, and he guided us to a tent where there were chili dogs and drinks being given out freely. Trail magic! The

Class of 2020 had come to Newfound Gap to encourage hikers who were following in their footsteps. It was a blessing to get out of the rain and feel the warmth of hot food radiating from my stomach through the rest of my body. The downs were becoming welcomed experiences. The trail was welcoming me, shaping my attitudes, challenging my old thinking, and rewarding me for simply walking her paths.

Before leaving Newfound Gap, I stopped in the restroom. It was warm and dry, so I hung out there for an hour or so. It gave me the opportunity to check the gear in my new backpack. When I began this adventure, I carried the pack that I had been using for several years. It was a sixty-five-liter pack made by Osprey. I really liked that backpack. It was comfortable, carried all I needed, and had pockets for everything. I knew where all my little things were kept, my first aid kit, headlamp, camera batteries, and the all-important toilet kit. It's funny how things become good friends while hiking. My only friend probably was its weight. At nearly five pounds, my Osprey was heavy. When completely loaded with gear, food, and water, she weighed in on the high side of thirty pounds. Those pounds begin to beat up my body as I climb up mountains and step-down rocks, which jar me from the soles of my feet to the top of my head.

Feeling a little like I had betrayed an old friend, I had a new backpack made by Ben McMillan, owner of Hilltop Packs. It was an ultralight pack that tipped the scales at slightly less than one pound. Ben had also made several other pieces of lightweight gear for me, including a food bag, fanny pack, and a little gadget bag to hold my electronics. Altogether, my new backpack weighed twenty-one pounds fully loaded. My back, shoulders, and knees appreciated the change. However, I was learning to trust this new gear. It is made of a lightweight, durable, water-resistant fabric called Dyneema. Would it keep my gear dry? I was especially concerned about my sleeping bag. If the bag's down stuffing got wet, it wouldn't keep me warm and night, and that could be dangerously bad on cold nights in the mountains. There are no electric heaters on the trail. We depend on our body heat to warm us after a cold day of hiking. A good sleeping bag and insulated air mattress are lifesavers, for real. I was relieved to discover all of my gear was nice and dry, protected by my new backpack. Warm, somewhat dry, and confident that my new pack truly had my back, I struck out climbing the path up and out of Newfound Gap.

The rocks were slick; the rain continued to fall, and the climb was taxing on my body. This was one of those ascents that seemed to have no end. The trail plays tricks on hikers. I learned to not look up when I was climbing toward the peak of a mountain. I might glance up long enough to pick a point to measure progress or a spot to break for a few minutes, but I refuse to focus on the challenge ahead. I simply looked at my feet and tried to keep from tripping over a rock or root and breaking my neck. However, there came a point that a quick upward glance revealed the blue-sky peeking through the trees. I excitedly thought, *It's over! I am reaching the top of this one!* However, I got there only to discover a sharp bend to the path that kept on climbing. This happened time and again. I was fooled by it every time too. The trail played that evil trick on me many times as I climbed up from Newfound Gap. Subtly, I began to realize that my attitude was being shaped by the trail. These experiences became funny, and I began to see how playful the trail could be with her guests who walked along her paths. Hard and challenging but inviting and rewarding too.

Finally, I began to descend to Icewater Spring Shelter. That would be my home for the night. Here, I encountered a different challenge that caused me to begin to reconsider how I would relate to the trail herself. The shelter was packed with hikers. The bubble had caught up with me. The impact of the heavy population on the trail was similar to a population explosion in a small town where the roads are not designed to handle so many cars. Most of the shelters in the Smoky Mountains are designed for up to twelve hikers laying side by side like pastries in a display case. Then there are a few tent spots, maybe four to six, for overflow. When the bubble collided with these areas, it was a nightmare.

Because of the cold driving rain, Icewater Spring Shelter was packed. There were probably thirty people in the shelter itself. Remember it is designed for twelve. Another twelve to fifteen tents were scattered around the area. The four level spots were taken, and I pitched my tent on the smoothest ground that I could find. However, the ground under me was slanted to the left, and throughout the night, my sleeping bag slid off the air mattress, and I would wake up trapped against the trekking pole that held up my tent. Fearing that the pole would fall and my tent would collapse on top of me, I tried to roll back onto the mattress. This would not be my last restless night because of crowded shelter areas. I was in the middle of the mass of hikers and didn't know how to escape it.

I want to take a sidetrack here for a moment. It is important to me that I point out most of those on the trail are friendly, welcoming, and hospitable. Just like the larger society, there are a few jerks, but they are rare and avoidable. It was wonderful to see so many people enjoying creation, walking on this old path, and seeking their own answers to why they were hiking. The demographic of these folks was broad and diverse. All ages, all ethnicities, and similar to my military experience, all welcomed one another. It renewed my faith in the future of humanity. It is a very different picture than we get from watching hate being sensationalized by the news media. I don't think the hiking community is a distortion of broader society. I think the distortions are created by news media pundits for their own agenda. Okay, enough of my soapbox speech. I wanted to let you know that I am not antisocial. I just needed solitude to discern answers for my own life, and the main purpose of my hike was to be alone and process a life of questions about the past, present, and future.

Back to the path. I left Icewater Spring early the next morning and continued to hike on the roller coaster of the Smokies. Ups and downs were followed by more ups and downs. The sun came out, and the weather was beautiful. It remained that way for the remainder of my hike through the Smoky Mountains. My body was adjusting to these mountains. I was embracing their challenges emotionally. I was beginning to get into a rhythm with the path as it unfolded before me. Suddenly and without any hint of its coming, a gap would form between the trees, and the trail rewarded me with a view of the mountains as they rolled upon one another. Row upon row, the mountains trailed off as far as I could see. The downs were as challenging as the ups, and it all nourished my soul.

Walking during the day satisfied my spirit while it depleted the energy from my body. I was alone with the trail most of the time. When I met other hikers, they typically passed me and were soon out of sight as if the trail had swallowed them up. However, in the evening, everyone reappeared at the next shelter. I arrived at Tricorner Shelter, and again, the daily traffic jam had settled in and welcomed me. More than forty tents were already pitched along the contours of the land. Only twenty or so folks were set up in the shelter itself. They invited me in, saying they could make room for one more. I appreciated their hospitality but declined and looked for a spot to pitch my tent.

In one of my many rest breaks of that day, I had met two guys about my age. One was a retired soldier like me. The other man looked to be a little older. We had had a good conversation sharing old war stories. By chance, one of them saw me as he was setting up his home for the night. He called out to say that they had saved me a spot for my tent. Ever so grateful, I quickly claimed the valuable real estate and began to make it livable for the night. Of course, the ground sloped down toward a large log. I thought that at least if I began to roll out of the tent, that log would stop me from careening off the mountainside. Little did I know that this was an idea that was nearly tested in the middle of the night.

I pitched my tent with my feet pointing downhill. Crawling into my sleeping bag, I thought that I would be more comfortable with my head perched higher. I had also taken the precaution of putting a thin foam pad between the tent floor and the bottom of my air mattress to keep the pad from sliding across the tent floor. It worked well, but I was surprised by a major flaw to my plan. About 2 a.m., I dreamed of falling off the bed and being trapped under it. When I woke, confused in my trance-like state, it became apparent that the satin fabric of the sleeping bag and the slick plastic of the air mattress were sort of like an ice cube on a countertop. Since I was on a slope, gravity had done its thing, and I slid off the end of the air mattress. I lay at the bottom of my zipped sleeping bag and was curled in a ball in the bottom. Like a person who had fallen through an ice-covered lake, I felt trapped and didn't know where up was. Fighting to free myself of this bag,

I finally found the zipper and rolled out into the cold night air. I laughed hard at my ridiculous situation but spent the next few hours sliding down, crawling up, and sliding down again. It was good to hear the birds waking up and finally start getting ready for another day of hiking. That concluded another restless night and began earnest plans on how to escape the bubble. It was a new experience in reality; *for every down, there's an up, and for every up, there is a down.* That maxim had crept inside my tent.

My journey through the Smoky Mountains was nearly over. I would have one more night to sleep in these old mountains. The past couple of days had been beautiful, and that beauty would follow me along the final section of this path. I walked out from Tricorner Knob Shelter with a stiff back, a little tired, and fully looking forward to the day ahead. There were a couple of substantial climbs ahead that would be followed by a long descent to Davenport Gap, the goal of today's trek. It was a fifteen-mile plan for the day, and I felt good.

As I walked along (and alone), my thoughts jumped forward to the evening. I had learned that Cosby Knob Shelter was closed due to "aggressive bear activity." In reality, it was closed because of negligent hiker behavior. A hiker had not used the provided cables to hoist his food bag up and out of reach of bears looking for some different cuisine. Instead, the hiker placed his food bag in his tent with him. Bears have a keen sense of smell, and they are very intelligent, maybe more intelligent than some hikers. So, smelling tasty treats inside, the bear invited himself into the hiker's tent to share a meal together. The hiker quickly exited his home for the night, and the bear made off with the food. So now rangers were on the lookout for the bear, and the shelter was closed to hikers. One of the consequences of all this was that hikers would now congregate into one shelter area instead of two. The upcoming Davenport Gap experience promised to be a repeat of Tricorner Shelter, if not worse. It was time to consider options.

I could try to push into Standing Bear Farm Hostel. That would be a nineteen-mile day. I felt good and could do that, but I wasn't quite ready to abandon the beauties of the Smokies. They had grown on me, and I was looking forward to one more night out here. I certainly didn't want to chance Davenport Gap. I had talked with several hikers who passed me during the day. Most mentioned that shelter as their goal for the day. So what was I going to do?

Looking at Guthook, an app that provides GPS location of where I am on the trail and lots of information about the various points along the path, I began to look for alternatives. Then I saw it! There was a blue blaze between Cosby Shelter and Davenport Gap Shelter. Blue blazes are side trails off the main Appalachian Trail, which is marked with white blazes. This particular blue blaze led to a fire tower on Mount Cammerer. The fire tower was built in 1939 by the Civilian Conservation Corps. It might be the answer that I was looking for. I have great respect for the young men who participated in the CCC during the Great Depression. It was one of Roosevelt's "New Deal" initiatives to offer work and skills training to young men in those desperate times. My dad had been in the CCC and had enjoyed it. At one point, according to NPR, the CCC operated eighty-four camps in North Carolina. We still benefit from their work.

I walked the seven-tenths of a mile off the trail and met a few day hikers who had visited the tower for the views. They reported that it was well worth the walk. They were right. It was perfect! The final quarter of a mile is a bit challenging. A rock scramble demanded visitors climb up, over, around, and through boulders to arrive at the two-story structure. The bottom section was filled with debris and junk. The upper floor offered a 360-degree view of the mountains and valleys as far as the eye could see. There were windows that surrounded the upper room, but time, wind, and vandals had broken most of them. They were covered with fabric and loose aluminum sheets that flapped, banged, and rattled in the relentless wind. An outside walkway encircled the exterior of the second floor. The view from that walkway was breathtaking. The sky was blue with a few white puffy clouds, and the mountains and valleys were endless. It was like the Smokies had saved its most spectacular self as a reward for my last night's visit.

I inflated my air mattress and placed the sleeping bag on a mostly flat, mostly level floor. All of my gear was arranged to dry in the safety of this old structure. Some folks had made comments in Guthook about friendly rodents visiting them through the night when they stayed in this place. I enjoyed a restful night with no guests, friendly or otherwise. I watched the most mesmerizing sunset of this journey. The next morning, I got up and watched the lights of homes and towns previously hidden in the valleys and on the mountainsides. They now accented the topography like Christmas lights decorating the trees. The sky began to subtly change colors with hints of purples and blues, which gave way to pinks and yellows. The sun suddenly burst through, and morning welcomed the day with all its glory.

The day would be a constant descent toward the northern terminus of the Great Smoky Mountain National Park. In contrast to the challenging ascent from Fontana into the Smokies, this was a gift, a continuation of the gift the Smokies gave me as a farewell. It was a sweet adieu. This down was such a spiritual up. I felt guilty, though. I had complained about the Smokies for days, but the trail had taught me to embrace the ups and the downs. I learned that lesson, and now I realized that I loved this place.

It wasn't quite over, and more surprises were in store. I had planned to stay at Standing Bear until I met another hiker as I neared the end of the Smokies. We talked about our next plans. He was moving on past the hostel and staying on the trail. I asked if the hostel had Wi-Fi, and he thought it did, but it wasn't very good. He said that the sleeping options were a bunkhouse or tenting. Neither option really appealed to me. I really needed space to consider my options to escape the never-ending bubble. I wasn't sure what I would do, but it would not include Standing Bear Farm.

I dropped the second half of my Smoky Mountains Permit in the designated box as I exited the park. It was a sense of accomplishment and a feeling that my plans were about to take a significant turn. The lessons taught by the trail are life lessons. Every aspect of the trail, whether reward or challenge, is reflected in our everyday walk. We all encounter downs, followed by ups, followed by downs, followed by…well, you get what I'm saying. There are few flat areas in life. Few times when we are simply coasting along with little effort to move forward. Instead, we encounter the ups of life that offer happiness. We may enjoy new friends or familiar foods. We may appreciate comfortable homes or be pampered during a luxurious resort vacation. We may feel like we are on top of the world. Then "life happens." That phrase hints of some ominous calamity taking place to rob us of our happiness. It may be a fight with a friend or loved one. It may be bad news from a routine medical checkup. It may be the loss of a job, a home, or someone dear to us. The downs can be hard. Still, there is healing in this lesson from the trail. As hard as the down may be, an up is just ahead. Hold on and embrace life's path.

The trail taught me that ups and downs would come, and I couldn't avoid them. So I prepared. I climbed up slowly. I looked at the beauties and appreciated the rewards given from the mountaintop vistas. I still try not to take this for granted. Remember, even when you move on to other places, the beauty of that place is still there. Beauty remains. Beauty doesn't vanish just because I am not there to see it right now. This is important to hang onto during life's downs. The rigors of climbing the ups strengthened me and prepared me for the rigors of the downs.

The downs also prepare us for the ups. In the dark valleys of life, there are lessons to be appreciated. No, I don't enjoy the pain or grief that waits in the downs. However, the downs do prepare me to appreciate the beauties of the ups so much more. Strangely, the downs are a gift to me that reminds me how much I am blessed. As I began to embrace the ups and downs of the trail, I began to be joyful. I wasn't always happy. When I was soaked by the rain, pelted by the hail, frozen by the cold wind, I didn't say, "Oh, this is so much fun. I am so happy today!" No, I was miserable, to be honest. Still, I walked through it because there was joy in the harmony of it all. Joy is different from happiness. Joy enhances the beauties of the ups, and joy makes the downs bearable. Joy keeps me from getting stuck in either the ups or the downs. Joy helps us check the situation around us and adjust as needed.

CHAPTER 2
IF SOMETHING DOESN'T
FEEL RIGHT, CHECK IT

"What can go wrong, will go wrong."

—Murphy

I was hiking on Birkhead Mountain in the Uwharrie National Forest a couple of years ago. I was considering a long hike but had not decided on a location. So the nearby trails on Birkhead Mountain offered an opportunity to get out for three or four days to test my gear, myself, and consider various longer thru-hikes. On the second morning of this hike, while the sunrise was still a couple of hours away, the birds were not yet awake, but I was, and it was time to pack up, strike camp, and get on the trail. I carefully packed my gear in reverse order of how it had been arranged in the tent last night. First, my sleeping bag in the sack that would keep it dry from any threat of rain. Then my deflated and rolled air mattress, spare clothes bag, electronics bag, cooking kit, first aid kit, and finally, the tent was taken down and placed in its little compartment on the bottom of my backpack.

Using the light from my headlamp, I scanned the area to be sure that nothing was left behind. "Leave no trace" is another motto of the hiking world. It means that we should carry out whatever we bring in with us. Littering is a mortal sin among backpackers. Everything was cleaned up, and it was time to leave. All my worldly belongings needed to survive were safely tucked away. I slung the thirty-pound backpack over my shoulders, grabbed my trekking poles, and started up the path.

As I walked, there was a sharp pain in my shoulder. I began to be aware of my body as I hiked. Sometimes there was a pain in a knee or a hot spot on a foot, and other times it was the back or shoulders that cried out to grab my attention. Our bodies take a pounding going up and down rough paths. Constantly carrying my home strapped to my back probably doesn't help either. Today was different, but I couldn't quite figure out this pain. It was a sharp, digging feeling that didn't go away as I stretched out the other sore joints of my body. Had I injured my shoulder somehow? The pain was in a strange place, a little lower than my shoulder and toward my chest. I thought to myself, *Quit whining and keep walking. It will eventually go away*. It didn't go away but only grew more intense with every step.

After a couple of miles, I put my thumbs under the straps to pull forward for some relief. The pain shot through my chest. When I looked down, something didn't appear right. The straps should lie flat over my shoulders and across my sides, as they are attached from the upper to the lower part of the backpack. My right strap appeared twisted. On closer inspection, I realized the problem began when I slung the pack over my shoulders; the sternum strap (a small strap that connects across the chest to hold the shoulder straps in place) had twisted behind the right shoulder strap. I snapped it together, and the strap's hard plastic buckle turned under the shoulder strap and dug into my chest. This was my first lesson in "If something doesn't feel right, check it." Chances are if something doesn't feel right, there is a problem. The corollary to this lesson is, "If something feels right, check it because it may not be." In other words, check and recheck your gear.

I had endured a couple of miles of pain for no reason. Had I stopped and looked, then I could have fixed it and moved on. Simple right? These lessons have taken a long time for me to really learn. In fact, I continue to learn them. Just as it took 200 miles for me to begin to embrace the ups and downs of the trail, I am only beginning to embrace all of these lessons.

My sternum strap was only the first lesson of this "If something doesn't feel right" maxim. The next lesson would be more painful. Three of my brothers and I wanted to go to the Gila Wilderness in New Mexico. Earlier, I had announced my plan to walk the Camino de Santiago as a pilgrimage. Two brothers wanted to join me on that 500-mile walk across northern Spain. The Gila would be a hike to prepare us for the pilgrimage journey.

We traveled together in Rick's truck. Again, Rick is my brother who had reintroduced me to hiking. We enjoyed the long drive from north Alabama to New Mexico. We took turns driving and napping (though not at the same time). A year before, one of our brothers had died. Since then, we have tried to make an extra effort to remain connected. It wasn't an easy commitment, as we live hundreds of miles apart. Rick, Roger, and Jim live in Alabama but counties apart. Mike and I live in different states; he is in Florida, and I am in North Carolina. Rick and I hike, though he has much more experience than me. Roger and Mike are perhaps a little more quiescent.

We finally arrived and set up basecamp. Our first real hike would be a loop of about seventeen miles. We were slack packing, which meant carrying a small pack with a few snacks, a first aid kit, and water. It was an experience. We had to wade through three streams as we began the journey. We had not hiked together, so no one knew what to expect from the others. After a couple of miles, Roger had had enough. He turned back toward basecamp, where he took off his pack and never donned it again for the entire trip. While Rick and I were working with Roger to be sure he knew the way back, Mike took off carrying the maps of the area. We thought that he would wait at the first junction, but we were wrong. We finally caught up to him toward the end of the day.

Rick had taken a picture of the map, and that was helpful. He and I tried to guess what route to take at the various junctions. Sometimes we were right, and sometimes we realized that we had gone east when we should have gone west. We circled back and were satisfied that we were heading toward our planned destination. We finally caught up with Mike; he said that he had left candies for us as trail markers. We had seen a couple of pieces of candy, but I think there were some happy critters who found others before we saw them. Regardless, it was good to be reunited once again.

Mike had twisted his knee on the path. He was in pain and had lost a lot of giddy-up in his step. We finally reached the parking area alongside the road toward basecamp. Rick walked on to camp, got his truck, and retrieved Mike and me. Mike was now out of commission.

The next day, Rick and I had planned to continue a forty-mile overnight trip. It promised to be a lovely time; a big loop would take us to a hot spring where we would camp for the night before winding our way back to basecamp and eventually reunite with Roger and Mike. It was a wonderful trail and unlike anything I had seen before. We walked up through a gorge where the sides were formed by high rock cliffs. There was a small creek that ran along the floor of the gorge. I had to look straight up to see the sky and thought about potential flash floods should the weather shift into a storm. There was no way out, no way to escape to higher ground. Flashflood took on a whole new meaning. Thankfully, we enjoyed fair weather throughout the journey.

I also began feeling something strange on the bottom of my right foot. Perhaps it was a wrinkle in my sock. I ignored the feeling, and we kept hiking. After about eight miles, we stopped for a snack. Rick said that he felt bad that Roger and Mike were not with us. I agreed. We then began discussing alternatives that perhaps would allow the four of us to enjoy the trip together. Soon we agreed to return to basecamp early, leave the next day, and go to Carlsbad Caverns. We packed up our food and started retracing our path. The feeling in my foot didn't go away.

Roger and Mike were surprised when we showed up that evening, but they were excited when we suggested moving on to see the Caverns. I was surprised when I took off my shoe to discover a good size blister on the pad of my right foot. Taking my sewing kit and antiseptic, I sterilized the needle and thread before piercing the big blister and leaving the thread to act as a wick to slowly drain the painful wound. This was another installment in my lesson, "If something doesn't feel right, check it." It would not be my last lesson.

Senior Hiker 77 and the Cumberland Island Gang

One week before going to Amicolala Falls to start north on the Appalachian Trail, I was invited by John, whose trail name is Senior Hiker 77, to join him on a hiking trip at Cumberland Island, Georgia. John hosts a YouTube channel that I enjoy. His wit and wisdom come together to make his videos entertaining and informative. We had shared comments on our videos, and I jumped at the chance when he asked if I wanted to join him and several YouTubers for that hike.

Cumberland Island was a different experience than the ups and downs of mountain trails with which I am more familiar. I think the highest peak that we created was 200 feet. That was over an eight-mile stretch across the island. Joining this group of hikers was a thrill. Everyone was inviting and interesting. We enjoyed the scenes and comradery. The animal life was fun to see, feral horses, pigs, seafowl of all types, and armadillos—lots of armadillos!

One afternoon, IceBear, RVA Hiker Girl, Jason, and I decided to hike up to the First African Baptist Church. It is a little one-room building that was constructed in 1893. It had no electric or water service. A local community still used the little structure for weekly worship. Its other claim to fame is that this little church was the wedding site for John F. Kennedy Jr. and Carolyn Bessette in 1996. As we hiked through the marshy land on a narrow path that was barely passable in areas, I told Jason that my shoes might be wearing out. My right shoe felt like the sole was splitting from side to side near the ball of my foot. Something didn't feel right. We kept walking and toured around the pretty little church before we continued up the trail to the island cemetery to see it.

At the cemetery, we recognized the great equalizer that death represents. Behind the gated, wrought-iron fence were headstones of former slaves and the family members of the plantation owner, Robert Stafford. There were new headstones, and we learned that those who were born on the island were welcomed to return to their final resting place here. Large conch shells mysteriously lined the top of the fenced plot for the Stafford family. A little creeped out, we walked back to our campsite in time to see an amazing sunset across the water off the island's coastline.

Finally, in my tent, I took off my shoe to examine it. There was nothing wrong with the shoe, but I had failed to lace it securely that morning, and my foot had moved around all day long; once again, a large blister had developed. Once again, I would have to tend the wound and hope that it would heal before starting on the Appalachian Trail. Once again, I was taught the lesson—if something doesn't feel right, check it!

I wasn't surprised to learn that the Appalachian Trail had its own version of this important truism, and I soon learned it. After leaving Fontana Dam and grinding out the 3,000 feet ascent to the top of Doe Knob, I thought this was the most challenging climb of my hike to this point. I was thankful for my new backpack, but something still didn't feel right. The right shoulder strap was uncomfortable, and my back hurt in strange places. This second maxim was again calling, "Check your backpack!" I'm sure it called me by some rude names as well.

This is a good place to talk about using some common sense and how, in backpacking for miles and hours, even the small things can become big things. A sloppy pack with a couple of small knots or protrusions can be wearing after a few hours of rubbing against your body. When I shed the pack and rubbed my hand across the fabric that lay against my bag, I discovered the culprits were several hard knots. When I packed my cook kit into the new bag, it was placed toward the back, and the hard plastic cover for the little stove protruded outward. Repacking, I stuffed my sleeping bag, clothes, and tent against toward the backside. Then harder items were packed toward the front. Sliding the pack onto my shoulders, I also noticed the right strap tended to twist toward the bottom. After straightening and adjusting the straps, the backpack felt like a soft glove against my back. It was marvelous, and my satisfied body thanked me for listening.

The Spirit Journey: Back to the Trail

In the beginning of this book, I wrote that hiking is a whole person experience of the body, mind, and spirit. The trail teaches whole person lessons as well. Sore knees, shoulders, and backs and blistered feet are the physical lessons that say, "Look at what you're doing. Something is wrong." My mind and spirit had to learn the same things.

To begin a journey like this, I knew that there must be a deep reason to compel me to drive on when I wanted to quit. When those times came, and they would come, I began questioning myself, asking if my sixty-four (soon to be sixty-five) year old body would endure the daily pounding of the trail and what would motivate me to push forward. Mind games are part of any experience of endurance and challenge. What would be the purpose that would overcome when I was lonely, homesick, or simply tired of the boring and pointless ups and downs? When my spirit waned and strayed, what source of faith would sustain me? This journey was much more than a physical test for me. I really wasn't interested in breaking any records or competing with anyone else who had hiked the trail. I was seeking a personal goal of getting to know myself. I prayed that if I was alone with myself long enough, I might even like myself. My life had been a life of service to others, military, law enforcement, husband, father, grandfather. Yet, I wanted to know if I served out of a sense of obligation, or did I serve because service poured out of my heart as a natural part of who I am? Such a journey needed time, evaluation, and solitude. I needed those things to accomplish the hike that I wanted. This was more of a pilgrimage than a hobby or an adventure.

Perhaps I needed the physical reminders of sore joints and blistered feet to remind me of the mental and spiritual lessons. Early in the hike, the trail was crowded with hikers. By the time I stepped onto the approach trail, nearly 3,300 people had used the Appalachian Trail Conservancy's website and registered their intention to hike the trail in 2021. There were others who had paused their 2020 hike due to the COVID-19 pandemic, and they shared the trail with this year's group. There are estimates that another group, perhaps three times larger than other groups combined, was not registered but was also hiking. The trail was strained to accommodate so many people. It was a challenge that I had not considered.

During the day, others were never far away, and this crowded my spirit, as well as my body and mind. My spirit shook inside me and began to whisper, *This doesn't feel right. I need to check what is disturbing me.* People were constantly passing and being passed. Some wanted to walk together, and those clumps of trail friends added to the congestion on the path. However, it was the evenings when things got interesting. The shelters in the Georgia portion of the trail are spaced out at eight-mile intervals. That's a full day's journey when walking up and down the mountain paths. The shelters were generally filled with hikers by the time I arrived. That wasn't a concern of mine. I preferred my tent. However, the areas surrounding the shelters were strewn with tents. Little homes of all shapes and colors were crowded together with hikers. All were new to the trail, and many were new to hiking. These shanty communities made for interesting dynamics throughout the night. One young man in his early twenties was hiking with his mother. She was a quiet, patient lady. He was the opposite. Throughout the night, her son constantly zipped open their tent; at the top of his voice, he fussed about being uncomfortable and then zipped the tent shut. Soon, other hikers who were awakened by his antics began to shout for him to go to sleep. His tent was about six feet from me. It wasn't the most restful night.

Early the next morning, long before sunrise, I packed my belongings, strapped them to my back, turned on my headlamp, and returned to the trail. I wanted to escape. As I walked, surprised to be descending and crossing a stream, I thought the day was supposed to start with a climb out of the Hawk Mountain Shelter. After about a mile, I decided this really didn't feel right. When I looked at Guthook, the GPS app on my phone, it showed that I was walking southbound! Yes, I was going the wrong way. Had I checked much earlier, then I'd have saved myself a two-mile error. Turning around, I walked back up the way I had come down. Oh well, the trail was quiet, and the sunrise was amazing.

The trail continued to be crowded, especially in the evenings. Still, nothing prepared me for the Smokies. After hiking 165 miles, I arrived at the Fontana Dam, the gateway to the Smoky Mountains. The lake and dam are amazing sights. Fontana Lake was seen through the trees while descending into Walker Gap. At first, there were just glimpses of the water. The closer I got, the dam accented the beauty of the lake. It was a wonderful contrast of God's creation and human craftsmanship. Soon, I was walking across the dam and up the path to the southern entrance of the Great Smoky Mountains National Park.

After ascending the grinding climb from Fontana to the top of Doe Knob, the first camping area in the Smoky Mountains was the Birch Spring Tent Site. It is the only tent site in the Smokies along the Appalachian Trail. All other overnight spots are shelters. Birch Spring was a warning of things to come.

The tent site is marked with a familiar wood sign identifying the wayside stop. A side trail led down into a hollow where tents were everywhere. There was a pretty stream flowing through the midst of the area. Cables had been installed to aid hikers in hanging their food bags up for safe keeping from hungry bears and other critters. I had left my pack up by the trail, where there was a couple of flat tent sites. After surveying the possibilities down among the other hikers, I decided to pitch my tent up by the main trail. It was a good decision. The hum of the hiking crowd was muffled by the elevation where I had carved out a settlement for the night.

After a restful sleep, I struck camp early and started up the trail, checking my phone app this time to be sure I was going north. I enjoyed the path lit only by the light beam coming from my headlamp. Squirrels and other small animals rustled around the edges of the trail. I was a little more attentive to the sounds in case a larger animal might be foraging for an early breakfast. Black bears are usually timid, but it was early in the year, and a bear would likely be hungry after his long winter nap. So I began talking to all of creation, singing to the trees, and making noise to let all things know that I was coming up the trail.

Soon, the birds were singing; the sky began to open with its beautiful colors, and a lovely day unfolded before me. Hiking up the first big climb of the day wasn't so bad when I couldn't see it. Soon the sun had chased away the darkness, and I discovered a spot where the trees opened to fully display the surrounding mountains and valleys. A perfect place for breakfast. While sitting there, eating, and enjoying the view, a couple of fellow hikers walked by and commented on the great spot that I had discovered. I invited them to join me, but they were in a hurry to get on up the trail. Part of me was thankful for the solitude, but part of me was a little sad when they didn't want to take time and soak in this gift of the trail.

So many beautiful views rewarded me as I walked along the trail. I began to realize and was surprised by the realization that I was completing the ascents without constantly stopping to catch my breath. Either the ups and downs were getting smaller, or I was growing stronger. Perhaps it was a little of both. The hiking was more enjoyable. There were times when I was nearly alone, just the trail and me. I was picking up speed. Maybe, just maybe, I was getting my trail legs! Hikers generally get stronger as they hike. They walk more miles with less effort. This is referred to as getting our trail legs. The days were rewarding, but something kept stirring inside my soul. Something didn't feel right.

The stirring grew stronger throughout the last three nights in the Smokies. I stayed at Icewater Spring, Tricorner Knob, and Mount Cammerer. Each place offered its own twist on this lesson of feelings. Each opened a different perspective of the common theme. Each gave me what I needed to consider why I was out here and how to take the greatest advantage of what the trail offered.

Icewater Spring was true to its name. I hiked nearly eleven miles in the rain from Clingmans Dome to this shelter. I was cold and soaked. The weather turned from bad to foul in the final quarter mile before arriving at my home for the night. Temperatures dropped, and the rain began to freeze. Hail about the size of golf balls began to pelt me as I tried to hurry over the rocky and slippery trail to the shelter. I confess that it was sort of fun in a sadistic way. These are the things that make great stories for my family and friends. It's sort of like childhood stories of walking to school through the snow (which I never had to do). Finally, I arrived at the shelter and dashed into the open-faced structure to meet about thirty of my newest best friends.

Many of the shelters in the Smokies were built by the Civilian Conservation Corps in the late 1930s. They are constructed from stones and have three walls, with the front open to the elements and a fireplace against one of the side walls. A roof hangs over the open front to provide cover for a little area where counter-style tables and benches offer places to eat. On this day, cold and wet hikers were crammed together in every place where we could escape the rain. A young couple, the man's trail name was Spectrum, and I think his wife was Sarah, kept a fire going in the fireplace. They gathered wood, stripped the wet bark, and fed the flames that felt so good against the cold. They also kept the occupants rotating so the newest and wettest vagabond could stand near the open mouth of the fire for warmth and dry a little.

Hospitality was on full display at Icewater Spring Shelter. Folks shared stories of their day and listened to new experiences. They passed around whatever they had, sharing their food, drink, and other vices in which I declined to imbibe. They squeezed tightly together to offer space to anyone who wanted to sleep in the shelter. Through all of this, my introverted self was quaking with desire to escape to the quiet of my tent.

After four or five hours of these close quarters, the rain stopped. I darted out to quickly set up my shelter before the rain began again. Inside the tent, I changed into dry clothes that had been kept in the bottom of my backpack, protected in a small water-proof bag, and taken out only for sleep. The wool leggings, shirt, socks, and hooded fleece pullover felt wonderful. I slipped into my warm sleeping bag and quickly fell asleep. The background sounds of laughter and storytelling didn't disturb me at all. The thing that did interrupt my slumber was the slope of the ground. There were no level places in the area. So I slid to the left all night and woke up with my body wrapped around the trekking pole used to hold up that side of the tent. I feared knocking down the pole and causing the tent to collapse on me in the night. I carefully unwrapped myself from the pole, crawled back up on the air mattress, and drifted to sleep again. An hour later, I woke to discover the same dilemma with the pole as it was buried deep into my side. I was thankful when the birds began to call me back to the trail for another day of hiking.

The trail welcomed me with its familiar rocky ups and downs. The downs were just as challenging as the ups. Inside, I complained about the challenges of the Smokies and thought how good it would be to finally look at this part of the trail in my rearview mirror. Just as I was complaining, the trees parted and opened to a beautiful vista of the mountains. I felt guilty for speaking ill of this place. My breakfast window was filled with layer upon layer of mountains, the sun casting shadows from puffy clouds down into the valleys. Streams and lakes, farms and small towns were visible from miles away. Oh, how I would miss seeing these beautiful views. I realized that I would miss the Smoky Mountains. They demanded a toll to pass through, but the rewards were worth far more than the price paid.

One of the great rewards was Charlies Bunion. Here is an outcropping of boulders nested on a mountainside. From here, an unobstructed view of the ranges stretched out as far as I could see. Mountain peaks reached upward toward the blue sky filled with a layer of clouds. Spring was coming, and the trees were changing from sleepy winter brown to the living color of bright green. In the distance, the bluish mountains blended with the blues of the sky as if they melted together. Words fail to convey how beautiful it all appeared. My soul absorbed the tranquility like a long, cold drink of water from the streams along the trail.

In contrast to the solitude of the trail during the day, the crowds of the shelter areas were jarring in the evenings. Tricorner Shelter was my stop for the night. After twelve miles of hiking, I was tired and ready to eat dinner, set up my tent, and sleep. The sounds from the shelter area were early warnings of the congestion that lay ahead. Tents were being set up along the trail before the side path that leads down to the shelter itself. I walked down the path, and tents were scattered everywhere. I was surprised when one young lady called to me, "Monk, you're here! Just go to the shelter. It's full, but they'll make room for you." I didn't recognize her, but she knew me. That's the hospitality and generosity of this community.

I walked on, not intending to stay in the shelter but hoping to find a semi-flat spot for my tent. There were probably twenty hikers in the twelve-person shelter and forty to fifty tents strewn through the area. Perplexed by the situation, I heard two other hikers call out, "Hey, Monk! We saved you a spot. Come over here." I had briefly talked with these guys during one of our breaks earlier in the day. One was an army veteran, so we had shared war stories.

Very thankful for their consideration, I began setting up my little tent palace for the night.

My experience at Icewater Spring had taught me to consider how I wanted to deal with the slope of the ground as I erected the tent. Tonight, I would put my head uphill and feet downhill. That seemed to be a more comfortable arrangement. It felt pretty good as I crawled into the sleeping bag and drifted off into unconsciousness. After a few hours, I woke up from dreaming that I had fallen off a bed. In a daze and anxiety attack, I discovered my body was curled into a ball and trapped in the foot of the sleeping bag. Unable to find a way out, I began crawling about until the zipper was located and opened. Instead of finding myself wrapped around my tent pole, I had slid down off the bottom end of the air mattress. I laughed hard. I'm still not sure which was worse, waking with a trekking pole embedded in my side or stuck in the bottom of a sleeping bag. Regardless, it was another night of very little rest.

I was thankful to get back to hiking, but not sure how to manage another sleepless night if that was my fate at the close of this day. During my breakfast break, a ridge runner (ridge runners are persons who bring trail news out to hikers as we walk) stopped by to tell me that Cosby Knob Shelter had been closed due to "aggressive bear activity." Apparently, a hiker had kept his food bag in his tent. A bear considered that as an invitation to come in and join him for some dinner. The tent was destroyed, and the food bag was taken. I don't know if the destruction was caused by the hiker's quick exit or the bear. In either case, the shelter that would have been used by some of the crowd was no longer available. Sleeping with a food bag in bear country is not a good idea. It certainly fits into the lesson, "If something doesn't feel right, check it because it may be wrong."

My goal for the day had been Davenport Gap Shelter, about fifteen miles from Tricorner. Now I was faced with the strong possibility of another sleepless night and began to explore options. The Guthook app is a valuable tool for hikers. It indicates where I am on the trail using GPS. It also shows many other details, including shelters, water sources, and sites of interest along the way. I discovered Mount Cammerer Fire Tower was a recommended site about a mile off the Appalachian Trail. Comments about this fire tower spoke about the amazing views it offers. It was described as having "Great views and an interesting fire tower…serves as a wonderful lookout." There were a few comments from hikers who had spent the night in the tower. This promised to be the option I needed.

I walked down the path and met a few day-hikers who said that it was a lovely site. The trail soon disappeared into a pile of boulders. I assumed that my destination was over those rocks. As I climbed up, there was a glimpse of the white, two-story round building. Finally, ascending to the steps of the fire tower, I found my home for the night. The door was propped open; several windowpanes were missing and covered with fabric and sheets of metal that flapped, popped, and banged in the strong winds on top of Mount Cammerer. This was my final night in the Smokies, and they had truly saved the best for last. The views were indescribable. A 360-degree view of tree-covered mountains extended outward as far as I could see. Looking down in the valleys, I could see there were little communities, farmsteads, lakes, and creeks. The sunset was a precious gift. As darkness covered the land, the wind grew still, and all was peace. This was the experience that I craved. I was so thankful for the contrast and realized that sometimes we need to see what "right" looks like to discern the cause of what feels "wrong." A shoulder strap had been twisted and was digging into my soul. The crowds were drowning my need for solitude, and the opportunity for contemplation was held beyond my reach.

The following morning was like an exclamation mark punctuating this lesson the Smokies was teaching me. Before the sunrise, the valleys were scattered with lights from homes previously hidden by the canopies of trees. It looked like Christmas lights sparkling on the largest of trees. Then the sun came out from its hiding place. Once again, the darkness began to subtly change shades. Purple and blue hews hinted of things to come. Then pinks, yellows, oranges, and reds burst from the horizon into the sky and chased the darkness away. This was on full display from here on this fire tower. It was as if God was saying, "You think you've seen wondrous things? You ain't seen nothing yet!" I was blessed.

Retracing my way back over the rocks and boulders to a smoother path that led about a mile back to the main trail, I started north once again. It was a beautiful day. In fact, the past three days had been lovely. After a couple of easy miles, the sign to Davenport Gap Shelter marked yesterday's original goal. I turned and walked to see what I had missed. It was a lovely shelter, much like the others where I had stayed on this journey. Two-floor decks inside could comfortably accommodate twelve weary hikers. Probably twenty to thirty had been there last night. The fireplace was still smoldering, so I got some water from the nearby stream and drowned the remaining embers. The surrounding terrain offered no flat spots for tents. It would have been a miserable night had I come this way. I was thankful that I had stayed on Mount Cammerer.

Moving on, I passed a young man who was enjoying a breakfast break. Joining him for conversation, he said that he planned to keep walking for a twenty-five-mile day. Both of us were excited to be completing this major milestone. In a few hours, we would leave the Smoky Mountains. I mentioned my plans to stay at Standing Bear Farm Hostel for a couple of days. Something in the way he looked at me caused me to question my plans. I asked him what he thought about the hostel. He said, "It has bunk houses and tent pads. Both cost about the same because there isn't much difference between them. Everything is on the honor system there. You keep up with what you get and settle up at the end. It's sort of a hippy place." Those last words were the deal-breaker for me. I didn't want to stay at "sort of a hippy place." I translated that as a party place, and I yearned for solitude. One of the questions that I had learned to ask often was, "What are my options?" I quickly reassessed and decided to get a shuttle to a hotel.

The small black box labeled "Permits" marked the northern terminus of the Great Smoky Mountains National Park. At mile 238.9 from my starting point on Springer Mountain, I had arrived at the end of the Smokies. I hoped to walk two more miles to the parking lot and call for a shuttle. I was excited. Walking on, I began to hear voices. It wasn't an indication of a mental break; sounds and voices echo down the trail for miles. These voices began to sound familiar. Two children were running down through the serpentine path toward me. They were leading two dogs, and then I saw Pat.

Pat is a good friend who lives in western North Carolina. He had monitored my progress along the trail by watching the Garmin Mini satellite tracker that I wear on these long hikes. The Garmin uses satellite communication and makes it possible to text my family when I have no phone signal, and it connects to a website plotting my location on a map. Pat had been watching and planning to meet me as I came out of the Smoky Mountains; now, here he stood. It was a wonderful surprise. We talked and laughed as we descended toward the parking area. The trail followed a meandering stream flowing across and spilling down boulders to form waterfalls. The kids ran ahead and crossed the stream on flat rocks that served as steppingstones. New leaves covered the trees with the brightest green of the season. This was the experience that I loved.

We walked the last mile back to his car, where he gave me a huge chicken sandwich, fries, and a large drink. This was trail magic at its best, given by a wonderful trail angel and his kids. They drove to a local hotel and deposited me in my room for a couple of days. The trail provides!

My wife, Connie, had planned to meet me at Standing Bear Farm in a couple of days. I called to tell her about this latest change of plans. Now I was at a hotel instead of the hostel. She would meet me in two days. In the meantime, I rested, reflected, and reconsidered my next move.

I rested my body. One of the first things that needed to be done was to get clean. The bathroom had a deep tub, as well as a shower. After getting the water as hot as I could take it, the tub was filled, and I lay down to soak. The tension in my legs and back was drawn out into the water and washed away with the grime that covered me. The water turned brown from the dirt washed from my legs and feet. After a long time, I showered to clean off the remaining filth and felt semi-human again with fresh clothes.

Editing videos to upload to my YouTube channel is a great way to reflect. I watch the various snippets of video and stitch them together to retell the journey's story. It helps me recall little details that I might have missed or forgotten were even there. Editing can be tedious. There are errors, blurred shots, and duplications that need to be removed. Some scenes must be placed in a particular order to really share my point of view. Editing is also a lot of fun. My artistic side is invited to play with the more logical, process-oriented side. For me, this process is very relaxing and playful.

After a day and a half of rest and reflecting on my experience over the past 240 miles on the trail, I was able to consider what compelled me to be out here. I could partially answer the question of why this was important to me. First, the trail allowed me to unplug from many of my responsibilities at home. At least I could mostly unplug, but my mind often drifted back to family needs. Unplugging gave me the opportunity to have conversations with myself. I realized that my life had been dedicated to serving others—military, ministry, and family. I serve because that is who I am. However, I also serve because I fear what others think of me. In order to fill validated, I need to be needed. One way feels right, but the other feels wrong. Serving others because that is the heart that I am given is fulfilling and satisfying. There is a word for someone or something that fulfills the purpose they were designed to fulfill. The Greek word is *doza*, and it translates in English as "glory." On the flip side, it is draining and depressing when I serve from a feeling of obligation or concern of being judged by others. I realize that it is easy for me to slip from the healthy place of fulfilling my life purpose into being concerned about what others think about me. The healthy side embraces who I am. The unhealthy side strives to live up to someone else's expectations. Glory is healthy, but falling into self-doubt from fear of being judged by others is not good.

The trail had shown me the difference between what is beneficial and what is not. I would be walking and enjoying the hike, but when someone came up from behind, I always stepped aside for them to pass. I eventually realized that it was less about being considerate and more about being self-conscious about what they thought about my pace. I considered the broader question about why I was hiking in the first place. If I was doing this to prove something to others, then I needed to just stop. Such motives would only lead to disappointment and more emotional injury. If I was hiking for the reasons I had told myself and others, then this was a journey for personal enlightenment, and that was a worthy cause. I concluded that there were mixed motives that compelled me to hike. One motive was to prove to others that I was still fit enough to do it. However, that was a minor ambition. My primary goal was to spend time with myself, getting to know me and discovering if I like the person that I see in the mirror. As I considered this as my real goal, then I considered the possibility of reaching the goal while hiking through the crowded conditions that I had experienced throughout the Smokies. Something didn't feel right, and I had checked it to discover the problem. Now I needed a plan to fix it.

CHAPTER 3
BROAD, SHALLOW ROOTS
DON'T HOLD IN THE STORM

"When the roots are deep there is so reason to fear the wind."
(African proverb)

The unsung heroes of the trail are the maintenance volunteers. These are men and women who carry heavy chainsaws, cables, chains, hooks, and materials to clear the path for us hikers. The only payment those folks receive is the gratitude of hikers and their own satisfaction for caring for the trail that we all love.

I met one of those wonderful trail maintenance volunteers after going up and collapsing at the top of Jacob's Ladder. His trail name was Boss. The night before, David and I pitched our tents along the side of a forest road. David is an artist. He is responsible for my "Wandering Monk" logo and the other graphics on my YouTube channel. David wanted to meet and hike some miles together. We began at the Nantahala Outdoor Center and enjoyed the grand climb up and away from the NOC. Two days and two freezing nights later, we walked out of Stecoah Gap and immediately began climbing up Jacob's Ladder, a 700-foot ascent that appears to be almost vertical. I had left early that morning so that I could tackle this infamous landmark without being embarrassed by on-lookers. I made it to the top without meeting anyone or being passed by any turtles or snails that might be out for a morning stroll. My effort was rewarded by feeling the need for a large oxygen bottle. With pack off and food bag out, I tried to enjoy a hot breakfast of oatmeal and raisins with a cup of instant coffee that tasted like tree bark in hot water.

I had almost recovered my breath when Boss came walking southbound on the trail. His backpack was filled with four-foot timbers. He stopped and introduced himself as "just a volunteer." Trail maintainers are some of the humblest people that I have met. He exemplified that virtue. I thanked him for his dedication to the trail. He answered that he admired us hikers. As we talked about his background, David arrived. He had survived Jacob's Ladder in much better condition than me. I was impressed. We enjoyed visiting a while before Boss continued on down the path with his load of wood. He was putting in some steps near the top of the Ladder to prevent erosion.

Boss had moved to North Carolina, specifically here near the Appalachian Trail, for the purpose of caring for the trail and supporting the hiking community. As he shared his passion, it became evident to me that this was who he was; his personal values were on full display. His family had a history of caring for nature and others. His roots run deep into the wellsprings of caring for others. Boss is an inspiring man, although he will be embarrassed if he ever reads any of this.

I learned to appreciate the work of trail maintenance teams while I wandered other adventures long before stepping onto the Appalachian Trail. A key mission of trail maintenance is to keep the path cleared of fallen trees. They also repair and care for the trail with erosion prevention projects.

When trees fall in the forest, they seem to find the trails. Large tree trunks fall across paths and make them almost unpassable. Maintainers cut the downed trees and remove the obstacles from the pathways. It is a behind-the-scenes and often thankless job. As we hike, we quickly become very grateful for the hard work of those volunteers. Every trail has its own way of teaching us life lessons.

Blowdowns are a common scene on forest trails. Blowdowns are trees that have succumbed to nature's forces and heaved up from the ground and collapsed. It seems they have an affinity for falling across the paths that hikers walk. This can be a minor annoyance or a huge obstacle. I am amazed at the ability of a single storm to knock down huge trees that have lived for scores of years surrounded by so many other trees. Why now? What differentiated this storm from all of the other storms that had moved through this thicket? What was different about this specific tree that once stood proudly among its neighbors and now lies stretched on the ground across the way that I must pass? So many questions flood my mind each time I encounter a blowdown.

On closer inspection, the answer to my problem appeared to literally rise up from the ground. Tree roots of blowdowns are pulled out of the ground like plucking carrots from a garden. They silently stare out at all who pass by. The downed giant lies beside a large hole in the ground where its roots had grown to gather nutrition and once anchored the trunk and canopy that reached to the sky.

A single storm had not toppled the tree, but a series of things contributed to its demise. Rain and wind from previous storms softened the earth around the tree's root system. Erosion stripped away the soil and created cavities that weakened its foundation. A culminating storm moved in, and the soil was soaked by the rain; the tall tree was buffeted by the wind; the roots were proved insufficient support, and the tree tumbled down and lay in front of me, blocking the trail. I inspected the blown-down tree, and its roots looked like a tangled wooden web that had once crawled under the surface of the ground. The roots were spread out and twisted together to form a foundation that once held the tree erect, but now it lay on its side. The roots had spread out broadly from beneath the tree, but they had not grown deeply into the ground. Lacking depth to anchor itself, the tree was doomed to the external forces that toppled it. This was a life lesson that I had to literally step over if I wanted to move up the trail.

I began thinking about shallow roots when I started hiking along local trails. Walking around Brandt Lake on a rainy day, I noticed the water collecting on the pathway, seeping into the soil, washing it away, and undercutting the roots of some of the trees. I recalled our old biology textbooks from high school. We didn't have access to the marvels of computers and technology. Those books included a colorful drawing of a human skeleton with several plastic overlays depicting layers of internal organs, nervous systems, muscular systems, and finally, skin. Here on this path was nature on display. The rain waters beat down on me, pooled up, and ran down the path. The soil was cut away, and roots were exposed. The giant trees were laid low as if the layers of life were being revealed to me. Shallow roots had stretched out to hold in good weather, but when the storms came, the ground shifted. With no deep roots to weather the storm, the tree came tumbling down.

During my first getaway to Birkhead Mountain, a strong storm struck during the first night of the trip. The storm was the maiden test of my new tent. I lay there listening to the fabric rustling in the wind and waited for the rain to leak through the walls. After several hours, my anxiety eased as the storm passed, and I remained dry and secure. The next morning, blue skies greeted me, and the sun dried the tent's outside. Satisfied that my shelter had passed its first real test, I ate breakfast, loaded up, and started down the path. Soon, I discovered a tree across the path. Walking around it, I observed the phenomenon of the broad, shallow roots. Several more trees were lying on their sides as I continued down the trail. I learned the lesson of broad, shallow roots that fail to secure the tall, otherwise healthy, and beautiful trees. Other trees withstood the forces of rain and wind. Their roots ran deep into the ground to secure them. Taproots burrowed down to underground streams to sustain them in the dry times as well as hold them through the storms.

I witnessed the most vivid illustration of this lesson while hiking on a Wyoming portion of the Continental Divide Trail. It took this experience to really appreciate the lesson of broad, shallow roots failing to hold tall trees. My brother and I traveled to Pinedale, Wyoming, to hike a circular route from the Big Sandy Trailhead to the Big Sandy Lake, through Jackass Pass and Texas Pass, across the face of the Cirque of the Towers, and to a junction with the Continental Divide Trail, which led us back to where we started at the trailhead.

Rangers told us that a windstorm had come through a few weeks earlier, blowing down a lot of trees. Maybe that's why this area is known as the Wind River Range. On the morning that we were leaving, a group of trail maintainers was heading out to continue their cleanup efforts. Several things struck me about this group. First, they were all young. They appeared to be in their early twenties, and a couple of elderly thirty-year-olds were in the mix. Second, they were young women and men. The drive to care for the trail crosses both genders. Third, they were all volunteers. These were not professional National Park Service employees. Finally, they were carrying all of the gear they would need to do the work ahead. This was a wilderness area, so no vehicles and no power tools were permitted. Crosscut-saws, axes, machetes, ropes, and an assortment of tools were strapped across their bodies, along with their backpacks with food and sleeping gear to remain out on the trail as they worked. These young folks thanked us for hiking the area and cautioned us to be safe. We thanked them for their selflessness and the great work they were doing for the trail and our benefit. I was amazed by their attitudes.

Rick and I struck out across a fairly flat stretch from the trailhead toward Sandy Lake, where we would spend our first night. This section would go alongside the river and through a pine and spruce forest. Normally this would have taken about four hours to hike, but we had been warned to plan on it demanding much more time due to the trail being blocked by trees blown down by the storm. As we hiked along the path, the river flowed over smooth rocks on the right side of the trail. On the left side, amazing views of tall mountains peeked through the spruce trees. In front of us, there were signs of the storm that had passed through the area. Taken all together, it was beyond anything that I had ever seen—breathtaking beauty.

After the initial walk into the area, we were not hindered by blown-down trees for the next couple of days. Much of the time was spent above the tree line as we transited Jackass and Texas passes. Each took us to elevations well above 10,000 feet. Tired but thrilled by these new experiences, we camped with the Cirque of the Towers as our back porch view.

On the final day of this adventure, we walked by several glacial lakes until we came to the trail's junction with the Continental Divide Trail. We followed the CDT going southbound and soon entered the pine and spruce forest. It was here that we were shocked to discover the epicenter of the devastation of the storm that so many people had warned us about. We made our way over or around several huge spruce trees that spread out on their sides and blocked the path. It was challenging but passable. Without warning, we discovered trees lying on their sides and extending far out to the left and right, blocking the trail. Trees were stacked on top of one another twenty feet high. It was a formidable obstacle.

We worked our way through a two-mile section of this wreckage. Climbing over or walking far off the path to get around the trees slowed our progress. Then, when we didn't think things could get worse, the trees were so densely packed together that we couldn't see our way over or around. Rick went to the right, and I went to the left. We were in search of an opening. We both found ourselves crawling under the trunks that lay prone before us. I had to take off my backpack, push it ahead of me, and crawl toward little openings that revealed themselves as I drew near. Eventually, we both made it through at about the same time. Calling for one another, we were soon reunited. It was intimidating for me. Here we heard the trail screaming its lesson—broad, shallow roots don't hold in storms.

My experience with the Appalachian Trail was different. I encountered fallen trees, but not to the extent of what Rick and I had witnessed in Wyoming. The efforts of maintenance teamwork were evident. There were several places where freshly cut wooden carcasses lined each side of the trail, but the path was clear. The trail is so dense in places that it is affectionately called "The Green Tunnel" by hikers. This is especially true in the Smoky Mountains portion of the trail. It was here that a unique perspective of the shallow root lesson was revealed to me.

The main learning point warning of the limitations of shallow roots was as true in the Smokies as anywhere. However, a corollary of that important maxim was equally proper. Fallen trees serve an important role in the ecosystem of the forest. These trees have many names. Sometimes they are referred to as "snag" or "snag trees." However, I have heard them called "Life Trees." I like that much more. These trees continue to serve life-giving purposes nourishing the forest. Rabbits, squirrels, birds, and even bats use the downed trees for homes and food storage. Bugs and fungi feed on the decaying wood. Even in death, these trees offer life to others. As I walked toward the top of Clingmans Dome, bright green moss covered the tree trunks that lay scattered alongside the path. It was the most beautiful five miles of the trail that I had seen so far. I was reminded all things have value during their lives and even after. Sometimes our greatest value may be pointing others forward along the path. Perhaps there is even hope for me.

CHAPTER 4
FOLLOW THE BLAZE

"Two footsteps do not make a path."

—Nnedi Okorafor

On the very first day on the trail, we arrived on top of Springer Mountain and met a young man who was sitting near the edge of the summit and taking in the beautiful scene laid out before him. It was the first of many similar views offered by the trail. Row upon row of mountains extended as far as the eye could see. The bluish traces of mountain peaks rose up and eventually disappeared into the blue skies that appeared to swallow them in. Between the mountain ranges were the forested valleys shaded in patterns by the sun's rays passing through the clouds above. It was beautiful.

Something seemed off with the young man who sat before these wonders. He was pleasant and engaging. He even offered to take my picture by the bronze plaque that marked the southern beginning of the trail. As we talked, he shared that he planned to stay in shelters throughout the hike. He had no tent, little food, and little of anything else. He had not planned for the journey beyond his desire to hike the trail. We parted company as I walked on up the trail, and he returned to his spot to admire creation. I never saw him again, and he remains in my mind even now. Planning is an essential part of hiking; even short hikes demand planning. It seems like the commonsense thing to do, but my dad often said, "Common sense ain't so common."

Planning isn't something that we do and then stop as we step out onto trails. We continue to plan, constantly assessing, adjusting, and making new plans. It was what I did while on active duty in the army. I was a planner. We created plans to accomplish an objective, but we also created branch plans in case we ran into problems, and we always ran into problems. We had sequence plans for those rare occasions when our plans worked, and we could push on to the next goal. Plans are living things; at least good plans are living things, constantly changing according to the realities of situations. The young man who sat on top of Springer Mountain didn't appear to have a plan beyond walking north. It is a dangerous thing to face the realities of the wilderness unprepared. The trail is a master teacher that prepares us to experience her marvelous treasures. However, good students of the trail follow in the steps of those who have successfully gone before us. They have marked the way. We share in their success when we follow their blazes.

Blazes are marks and symbols that are usually painted on trees along the path of a trail to identify it. Somewhat like street signs, different trails may be identified with different blazes. The Pinhoti Trail through Alabama and Georgia is marked with signs of turkey footprints. The Benton MacKaye Trail is marked with a white diamond shape. The Appalachian Trail has white rectangular blazes about the size of a dollar bill. These blazes reassure hikers that they are on the right path. Remaining on blazed trails is critical. Every year, a few hikers get lost by stepping off the path. They may step away to attend to bathroom needs, walk a few hundred feet, become disoriented as the forest door closes behind them, and they can't find their way back. It is a frightening and sad reality. There are solutions to prevent these unfortunate situations. Poor planning ignores the potential perils of the trail.

Blazes show us the way if we will follow them and when we can see them. Snow, rain, darkness, or other distractions cause us to miss the blaze. It's easy to get turned around and go south when I should have gone north. There are other tools available to help hikers. Modern technology has given us interactive tools for our smartphones. Satellite communication devices like my Garmin are tremendous aids to keep us from losing our way. However, the blaze remains the greatest marker that others have gone this way before me, and they continue to show me where to follow in their footsteps. The blaze, that small mark alongside the path, is a great comfort every time I see it.

Early in 2020, many hikers were getting off trails at the advice, even coercion, of trail conservancies and hiking associations due to the coronavirus pandemic. My plans to walk the Camino de Santiago were scraped due to travel restrictions. Feeling trapped by forces beyond my control, I sought escape. When a friend told me about Birkhead Mountain, it felt like the chance to breathe again. The blaze introduced itself to me on that old mountain.

My plan was to hike a circular path around Birkhead. It was a three-day, two-night adventure. Just a break from the claustrophobic constraints that were pressing in on me. Connie drove to the trailhead about an hour from our home. She was a little concerned that I would be arrested for "breaking the rules." Personally, I really didn't know what to expect. We had never experienced these restrictions to going anywhere in America. After all, we lived in "the land of the free." Perhaps this added to my growing anxieties at home. That all changed on the trails there at this old mountain, which welcomed me into its trees and streams.

I met a young family who had come out for the day. The father had grown up in the area and knew the paths. We chatted and shared our dismay about what was going on around us. Then we moved down the trails in separate directions. It felt good to be alone and outdoors. The well-worn trail was easy to see. Although I had never been there before, my phone had an app called AllTrails, which displayed a map of the trail and an arrow indicating where I was on that map.

The second morning, after packing up all of my gear, I started down the trail. The blazes on the trail were similar to the Appalachian Trail blaze. They were white rectangles about three inches wide and six inches long painted on trees alongside the path, similar to the blazes marking the Appalachian Trail. However, I often looked at my phone to reassure myself that I was on the right way. My phone reassured me, especially at trail junctions.

Eventually, I came to a junction where the blaze indicated the main trail turned off to the right. However, the AllTrails app on my phone directed me to go straight. Trusting technology more than paint, I followed my phone. After a mile, the path became overgrown. Thinking that it had probably not seen much traffic, I continued hiking down the trail. Soon, it stopped at an old cemetery. My trusted phone was not so trustworthy. Turning around, I walked back to the junction where the blaze looked as if it was smiling smugly, mocking my mistake. I was introduced to the maxim, "Follow the blaze and listen to those who have traveled the way before." Learn from their mistakes and don't repeat them. It is an important lesson for hiking new trails, as well as our journey through life.

These lessons often repeat themselves. They underscore their importance on other trails, especially for those who are slow to learn like me. During a different outing, the trail emphasized the importance of following the blaze. I planned to hike a segment of North Carolina's Mountains-to-Sea Trail. That portion of the trail stretched along the Dan River from Hanging Rock to the town of Danbury.

Beginning from the parking lot of the visitor's center, I began to ascend Hanging Rock. There are a series of waterfalls just off the trail. Each waterfall is marked with a little directional sign that includes the name of that particular waterfall. Visiting each one, I was especially intrigued with "The Hidden Falls." The water flowed down the river and disappeared under a pile of large granite rocks. There were gaps and openings among those boulders where I could stand on top and look down to see the waters cascading beautifully over a ledge and hear the roar of the falls. It was really a unique and beautiful sight. I stood there for a long time, almost hypnotized by the view. Eventually, something shook me from my trance, and I realized that it was time to get back to hiking.

Something was wrong as I began to hike. I had followed blazes to get to this point, but now I couldn't find the blaze that should direct me onward. There was a pathway through the growth of weeds, bushes, and trees. Deciding to walk that way, I was sure that a blaze would soon greet me. However, in my haste to push forward, I forgot that the trail was actually behind me. I had walked a side trail to get here, and my mistake would create challenges, potential dangers, and amazing treasures.

Continuing to walk on the unmarked path, I realized this was not part of my plan. This portion of the Mountains-to-Sea followed the Dan River until it ran out of the park. My new direction was taking me away from the river and up a mountainside. It was a clear path, but the wrong one. One of my many weaknesses is that I don't like to go backward. That personal flaw had contributed to this challenge, and it would continue to aggravate it. I could hear the river flowing below and knew that I was far off the trail that I wanted. I could have and should have retraced my steps back to the correct trail and continued on the way. But no, that would have required me to go back! So, in my foolishness, I decided to bushwhack. Bushwhacking requires cutting a new path through the forest, and this was a dense forest with young trees tightly packed together, thickly covered in briars to make things interesting.

As I walked toward the sound of water, the challenging path tore at my clothes and skin. I lost my favorite hat that had been given to me by one of my brothers. Still, the roar of the river beckoned me in the right direction to the proper trail. Bushwhacking creates potential dangers. I walked through the thick brush, and my feet disappeared in the undergrowth. Briers scratched at my legs and arms; vines grabbed at my body as they attempted to hold me back or trip me up. Progress was slow and difficult. However, the thing that was most unsettling was the absence of a trail. There was no evidence that anyone had ever been this way before. No blazes marked a path, and there was no path to be marked.

Pushing my way through the forest growth, I stepped carefully to feel for the ground. Hidden rocks or roots added to the hazards. Then, I stepped onto the top of some tall grass and briers. As my foot descended toward the ground, it continued downward. I felt no solid ground where I thought there should have been solid ground. Pulling my foot back to safety, I parted the underbrush with my trekking poles and gasped at the view. The reason I hadn't felt solid ground was there was no solid ground. The vegetation had hidden a sharp cliff edge. Had I stepped off that ledge, then I would have fallen about fifteen feet down to the bottom of a gorge. Blazed trails can save hikers from many potential dangers.

There are challenges and dangers that threaten hikers who leave the marked paths of the trail. However, there are also amazing treasures hidden in the dense bush of the forest. After my near disaster, I stepped back and sought a safe way to descend the cliff and move down toward the river that continued to signal the way by its roar. In the middle of all the growth, there was a small circular opening that was about ten feet in diameter. In the middle of that opening, a baby deer lay curled up. The little fawn appeared so peaceful as she slept on the soft grass, completely unaware that I was there. Perhaps her mother was out foraging for food and had tucked her little one into this nursery in the forest for safety. I took a couple of pictures and, as quietly as possible, exited the area without disturbing the little one. I remembered the first time I had seen my daughter when she was born, so peaceful, so precious. Seeing the fawn ranks among the greatest treasures that I have witnessed in all of my hiking adventures.

Whether simple rectangles, diamonds, circles, or more elaborate replicas of animal footprints, blazes offer security and reassurance. Blaze-marked trees tell me that others have passed this way. Others who were more experienced and wiser than me marked the path so that I can now share in their experience. What about trails where trees are few, or there are no trees at all? On the Appalachian Trail, sometimes blazes are painted on sidewalks when the trail passes through a town. They may be painted on bridges or boulders to show the way over rock scrambles. However, when Rick and I hiked through a segment of the Wind River Range in Wyoming, we encountered a very different terrain. Over much of our adventure, there were no trees.

On the second day of that outing, we began to ascend the mountains. We ascended elevations more than 11,000 feet. We were far above the tree line, and the rocky terrain was like walking on the moon. The air was thin and cool. The views were clear and spectacular. The experience was spellbinding. The climb had demanded all that I could give, but it was more than worth it. However, we encountered a challenge that I had not considered. There were no blazes! There were no marked paths either. The hard, rocky surface resisted wear, and few hikers visited this area to wear a path anyway. We learned to rely on two tools to find our way.

The first tool we discovered in the mountains was cairns. Cairns are sort of like blazes. They provide landmarks to show that someone has been this way before us. Cairns may have different meanings and serve different purposes. They have a deep history. Cairns are basically rock piles of many different sizes and are usually stacked to form sort of a peak. The word "cairn" is Scottish, and burial cairns are well known in Scotland. Native people of North America also used rocks to identify burial sites. Among hikers, cairns are used as navigational aids to mark key terrain. Sometimes, trail blazers use these rock towers to mark a trail; sometimes, hunters use them to mark hunting areas that have been scouted out for game. The point is that cairns can be misinterpreted, especially by the uninitiated hiker who doesn't know the area. This was my problem. We saw the familiar rock piles but didn't know how to interpret their purpose. They were few and far between, and the locals talked of hunting throughout the mountains.

My second tool, which was much more reliable here, was my familiar hiking app—Guthook. While we were home, I had purchased the Guthook maps of the Wyoming portion of the Continental Divide Trail. The app enabled me to find that Sandy Lake section of the trail and then customize a route around Sandy Lake, through Jackass and Texas Passes, over to the CDT, and return to the original trailhead. Then the GPS tracking ability of Guthook guided us along that route. Frequently looking at my phone, we knew if we were on the trail or if we had strayed off and were in danger of becoming more lost than we felt we were much of the time. I never considered what would happen if I had lost or broken my phone. Let's not think about that now.

Technology often proved itself to be our friend. There was a portion of the trail through the Wind River Range where Rick and I had been climbing up a boulder scramble for what seemed to be more than half of a mile. When we got to the top, we were surprised to discover a sheer edge—no path led further along the way. I consulted Guthook, and it showed that we had veered off the trail by several hundred feet. Yep, we turned and retraced our steps to descend back the way we had come. Halfway down, there was an opening through the rocks toward where we needed to be. So we walked through that little pass, found the way that we should have gone, and once more struck out through the mountains. Eventually, our eyes seemed to recognize the pathways through the mountains. They often revealed themselves just when we needed them. I thought of the *Indiana Jones and the Last Crusade* scene where Harrison Ford appears to step out into the open abyss and feels the bridge under his feet. The trail sometimes reveals herself when we need it. That also taught me another lesson about trust, but I will share that in a later maxim.

The Appalachian Trail is well marked. White blazes mark the main path, and blue blazes indicate side paths to water sources or other sites of interest. Charlies Bunion and the fire tower at Mount Cammerer are found on blue blazes. Wooden signs are engraved with directions at junctions with other trails and paths down to shelters. The trail is well marked, but we need to know how to read the blazes. There is sort of a code. The color is an easy reminder that there is something different about that trail. Other codes involve blazes over blazes. Walking along and seeing a blaze with a second blaze hovering over it is like a warning sign saying, "Turn ahead!" or "Intersection ahead," and it tells hikers what to do to stay on the path. These are especially helpful when the path appears to go straight, but that is actually a clearing for erosion control or a pathway for maintainers to preposition materials for a future project.

Often, the blazes were just on top of one another, and that was useful. I knew there was something ahead of me, and I would need to make a decision, but the signage did little more. It's sort of like the warning signs that say, "Lane closure ahead." I despise those signs! I want to shout, "Okay, which lane is closed!" No one knows until we crawl forward enough in the traffic jam to see that we have indeed chosen the closed lane, and no one will let us move over into the clear one. There are no traffic jams on the trail, except maybe at the shelters, but it is nice when the blaze offers a little more information. When the top blaze is offset to the right of the bottom blaze, hikers know that there is a right turn ahead.

When the top blaze is offset to the left, then we are going to turn toward the left. Pretty simple and very helpful.

Those who have walked these paths before me thought of me and marked the trail. I enjoy the sights, sounds, and experience of the route that others have created and maintained for me. When I listen to others who have gone before and follow their blazes, then I enjoy the fruits of their experiences; perhaps I avoid their mistakes rather than repeating them. Blazes are little things that represent a huge commitment by many others, and I reap the reward of their labor. The trail has taught me to appreciate the little things.

Chapter 5
Bigger Isn't Better

"Love measures our stature: the more we love, the bigger we are.
"There is no smaller package in the world than a man all
wrapped up in himself."

—William Sloane Coffin

My wife has often said that I am a "big thinker." That is a kind way of saying that I am a dreamer. She is right. As a young boy, I dreamed of big things. Growing up in rural Alabama, I was never confined to a small space. My brothers and I could roam free without fear. We probably were naïve to the real dangers that lay in wait for unsuspecting little boys. We rode our bicycles for miles and miles down country dirt roads, through open fields, and along paths through the woods and pine thickets that surrounded our little home on the hill. We explored narrow caves that we discovered, swam in creeks and streams, and hunted squirrels deep into the forests. We dreamed of being race car drivers, brave soldiers, and famous explorers. Our dreams were as big as the outdoors, where we lay on our backs and stared at the clouds and stars high in the sky. Regardless of what we dreamed, big seemed to be great!

The trail has a way of tempering my hunger for big things. Perhaps immersing me in its deep forests and rows upon rows of mountains, the trail is schooling me in an important lesson—bigger is not always better. As I slow down enough to see an industrious spider or a fluorescent green tiger beetle or a scampering squirrel, I become less focused on myself. Sometimes I pause from looking at the distant beautiful mountain ranges and see the blackberries, huckleberries, wild strawberries, or the fruits of maintainers' labor on the trail herself. The evidence of their presence is everywhere. Tree trunks are moved or cut to open the path once again. There are rock steps to ease a steep incline or logs partially buried to divert rain waters over the mountainside rather than down the trail. These apparent "little things" offer great rewards. No, bigger isn't always better. Often, the little things accumulate and contribute to big outcomes.

My dreams of hiking long trails were born from Tom Schmidt's stories. Tom is a good friend. He began telling me about his journey across Spain on the Camino de Santiago. Tom had recently retired from his medical practice and now had the opportunity to complete this pilgrimage. He shared stories about going over the Pyrenes Mountains from France into Spain. He described the towns and villages along the way. The historic churches built by Templar Knights are scattered along the trail. Various statues and other artwork welcome pilgrims. There is the desert where the journey transforms from a physical exercise into a spiritual awakening. The *crème de la crème* is the Santiago Cathedral. This old church is the legendary resting place of Saint James. I wanted to fly to Spain right then. Tom counseled me to prepare for the experience. He gave me books to read and websites to study. I soaked it all in and reserved my airline tickets and even space at the first hostel in the Pyrenes. All was set until the coronavirus pandemic brought the world to a stop. So rather than the grand adventures of a 500-mile thru-hike, I turned to local trails.

The local trails were three-to-fifteen-mile day hikes. They weren't grand multi-day adventures like Tom had described. I walked them as a disappointing consolation to bigger dreams. However, each trail began to reveal beauties. Several trails surrounded Lake Brandt near my home. They had fun names like Bald Eagle, Nathaniel Green, and Long Trail (which isn't very long at all). Each offered a different view of the lake, and combined, they offered a full day of hiking. I learned to use my trekking poles so my hands didn't blister from holding them too tightly. I learned to walk across paths covered with webs of tree roots so that I didn't twist my ankles. I learned to carry enough water but not too much. Each outing provided me with a new lesson. Each hike prepared me for something bigger. I learned to love these trails as much as any others.

The Appalachian Trail was my next big dream. Missing the chance to walk the Camino in Spain, I wanted to take on the nearly 2,200 miles of the trail from Georgia to Maine. This was the grand challenge, the big goal, and I wanted to claim it. So my local hiking routine remained the same. I did begin researching and planning for the logistics necessary to hike the AT.

It's one thing to hike twenty miles in one or two days a week, going home at night to dinner, rest, and sleep in the comfort of my bed. It's another thing completely to hike through the ups and downs of the mountains daily for five or six days before stopping to resupply, take a much-needed shower, washing your only shirt and pants, and getting back out for another five or six days. The little things add up and drain the body. Friends would come out to hike a section with me, but we had very different goals. It's one thing to plan on hiking thirty or fifty miles and then go home. One can push themselves, knowing they will soon be able to go home. It is entirely different to plan on hiking one or two thousand miles that will take months of steady walking up and down these pathways carrying your home on your back the whole way. The little things cannot be avoided on long hikes. Cold and heat, drought and storms will come. They are unavoidable. We learn to embrace it all.

When I began hiking north from Springer Mountain on the trail, the weather was amazing. I began hiking from Mile Zero on March 9th. It was still winter, but it felt like spring. The temperature was perfect, and the skies were blue and dry. I enjoyed seven days of beautiful, rain-free hiking. During one video, I remember asking, "Can I get through Georgia without getting rained on?" Mother Nature was listening, and she responded on day eight with a resounding, "No!" Mike and I had stopped at Low Gap Shelter for the night. The shelter area was sort of crowded. The little shelter could comfortably sleep six, but eight hikers had arranged their nests for the night. Mike was number eight and was making room for me, but I declined. It seemed too crowded. Of course, I hadn't seen crowded yet. Anyway, I pitched my tent near a wonderful stream that provided water to thirsty wanderers. I was sleeping comfortably when my tent was lit up by lightning, followed quickly by a crash of thunder. The storm had arrived, and the rain pounded heavily on my thin tent walls. It was the first storm that I had experienced in this tent, and it proved itself to be a trustworthy shelter. What a relief.

It was early; there were no hints of sunrise, and it was raining. So I packed my gear and strapped my tent on top of my backpack so that its contents remained dry. Striking out on the trail in the storm, I enjoyed the experience. These were bragging rights for stories that would be shared back home. For much of the day, the rain continued to soak me. Thankfully, everything inside my pack remained dry.

Around 2 p.m., the rain eased to a near stop. I took advantage of the opportunity to have some lunch. There was an opening with a log laid alongside the trailway. It was far enough off the path that I could sit and not block others who would pass me. Sitting on one end of the log, I made my usual noontime meal from a small tub of peanut butter, a package of honey, and a tortilla. These peanut butter burritos are a favorite staple of mine. As I sat there, a small squirrel jumped on the other end of my organic bench. He didn't seem to care that I was there at all. In fact, he chirped as if we were to have a conversation. I talked with the squirrel, and he chirped his responses. Finally, I sat the partially empty peanut butter tub between my friend and me. He soon crawled to the container. He didn't scamper off with it as I had anticipated. Instead, he sat and cleaned the tub of its contents, chirping with me all the while. After thirty minutes, maybe more, the rain began again. My little friend and I said our goodbyes. I cleaned up the trash from lunch, including the now empty peanut butter tub, and once again started north. I enjoyed many meals with beautiful views, but that meal with the little squirrel was my favorite of the trail. Big things are not always better. Often little things tell of great things to come.

Early in April, spring was beginning to show itself. Tree limbs were covered in buds where leaves would soon burst out with the greenest green of the year. Clumps of grass sprouted from the sides of the path. And the April showers gave drink to the coming May flowers. I was walking from Yellow River toward Fontana Dam. The trail's familiar ups and downs kept me alert for loose and slippery rocks, which were plentiful through this section. I didn't look up much because the treacherous trail demanded my full attention. However, as I was looking at the path before me and discerning the best way to go around or over the rocks and boulders, I was stopped by one little sight. I hadn't seen the beautiful vistas of mountain tops extending to the horizon or the beautiful valleys that were beginning to change to green from the trees and grasslands. The sight that caught my attention was a little sprig of a flower pushing up through brown leaves. I don't know why my eyes were drawn to this single little hint of life, but I stopped and kneeled down to get a better look. The little plant looked so vulnerable and small, but on its top was a blue bloom. The petals of the bloom appeared as vulnerable and small as the stem they rested on. After several minutes, it was time to move on. As I began to stand up, my eyes fell upon the field of tiny blue flowers that stretched out under the trees and far out to the ridge of the hill that I had been walking alongside. In my quest to see the big things, I nearly missed one of the most mesmerizing views of the day, a patch of the smallest blue flowers emerging from the leaves of the forest. It appeared as if they were singing welcome to life returning springtime.

My final day in the Smokies underscored this lesson that the trail was teaching me about how bigger is not the definition of better. Better can be found in many places, whether they are short walks, small flowers, or friendly forest critters. Sometimes better reveals itself in the contrasts between huge and not-so-huge. The night before walking out of the north end of the Great Smoky Mountains National Park, I had stayed in the fire tower on top of Mount Cammerer. The Smokies had given me a full display of her beauty. The mountains reached up and faded into the blue skies far out on the horizon. The green valleys concealed houses, farms, and villages during the daytime but revealed their lights in the darkness like stars on the ground competing with the stars in the heavens. The sunset and sunrise were breathtaking. The bigness of the mountains shouted for my attention.

The next morning, I hiked northbound. The sides of the path constantly opened to give glimpses and reminders of the vastness of these mountains. I walked out on one rock ledge to admire these beauties, but as I turned to get back on the trail, something caught my eye. It wasn't as small as my squirrel buddy, but it wasn't as big as the mountains either. It was a retaining wall built alongside this path. Constructed of cut granite blocks that were probably five feet wide and ten feet long, these blocks were skillfully laid upon one another like bricks on the side of a house. Building that wall had been no small task. It looked similar to the foundation of the Mount Cammerer Fire Tower, and I assumed it was another product of the Civilian Conservation Corps from the late 1930s.

The wall secured the side of the mountain, following the pathway for about a mile. It was slightly higher than ground level and went down the mountainside maybe ten to twenty feet. Without the wall, erosion would have washed the trail down into the valley far below. It was a strong contribution to maintaining the overall trail for nearly a century, and it looked like it would continue to protect the trail for centuries to come. Not only was it effective, functional, and durable, it was beautiful. The wall didn't stand out like some gaudy icon of abstract art. It blended into its surroundings and was almost unnoticeable. However, I had been fortunate enough to notice it. The gray stone, with its roughly hewn, was neatly laid. Again, I thought of eighteen- and nineteen-year-old men who had worked under the supervision of US Army Engineer Officers to accomplish this lasting task. I thank them all. It is one of the great stories of the Great Depression in United States history. Little things can have great impact. They can encourage us to continue steadfast on our journeys and to stay on the path ahead.

CHAPTER 6
STAY ON THE PATH

"Does the walker choose the path, or the path the walker?"

—Garth Nix

I usually end my videos with a common refrain, "Stay on the path!" Different people tend to interpret that little phrase differently. That is one purpose for saying it—to bring your meaning to mind. Some hear me saying, "Be careful to follow well-marked trails and not get lost." Others may hear another message that encourages them with a deeper understanding, "Embrace the trail for whatever it offers ahead of you." I leave the meaning for this saying up to the individual who hears it. However, most maxims are like icebergs. The tip is exposed, but the biggest part lies buried quietly beneath deep waters. I learned a deep lesson for myself in "stay on the path" while hiking over many miles and weeks when the physical demand gave way to the mental stress and looking at the rough paths of the trail turned inward to the uncharted paths of my soul.

Preparing to hike the Appalachian Trail, I read books, listened to podcasts, and watched videos—lots and lots of videos. I'm a big believer in learning from others. Seasoned hikers readily shared the lessons learned from their experiences. They discussed how to care for blistered feet, reliable gear and gear that failed them during their journey, the physical demands, and the mental stresses of long-distance hikes. They also answered questions and concerns about things not answered in their presentation. Popular champions of the trail were people with strange trail names like Darwin, Bigfoot, and Dixie. Their videos were well-edited and entertaining.

I had never done anything like this before, and my plan was to do it alone. I had many questions, but the most nagging thing was I didn't know what I didn't know. So books also helped me prepare. I read Michele Ray's *How to Hike the A.T.* as well as Chris Cage's book with the same title. Bill Bryson's *A Walk in the Woods* was a lot of fun, and David Miller's *The A.T. Guide* was the most useful reference book that I used during my hikes. These are all great resources, and I recommend them for anyone planning to hike anywhere.

Another valuable resource was those who were hiking the trail now! I began binge-watching videos of hikers who were literally stepping up to the challenge of hiking this unimaginable journey of nearly 2,200 miles. They tested their bodies, minds, and spirits. Their entire soul was pouring into the task of this adventure. My favorites were "Wild on the Trail," "They Call Me Hickory," and "Hiking with Braids." Each person I watched shared a very different view of the trail through the lens of their own personality. The way each one approached their experiences helped me anticipate the challenges ahead and consider how I would respond to the task of hiking.

Their videos reflected the people that I met during my own journey. Some enjoyed the awe of the trail, while others sought to conquer the trail. Some embraced the good and the difficult, and others found fault in every aspect of the experience. The people who step out on the paths of nature are as varied as the terrain we encounter along the way. The lessons they all taught me are summed up in my adage, "Stay on the path!"

The 604 steps ascending Amicalola Falls and the mountains of northern Georgia are real tests of endurance. They challenge the aspirant who steps onto the trail with the intent of walking its way for nearly 2,200 miles through fourteen states. The section between this beautiful waterfall and Bly Gap at the Georgia/North Carolina border is a microcosm of the entire Appalachian Trail. The challenging ups and knee crushing downs, rocks, mud, and scene after scene of indescribable beauty invite the pilgrim to push on through it all.

Many people end their hike before reaching this point. The famous "shoe tree" at Neels Gap testifies to those who quit after thirty miles and throw their hiking shoes into the branches of that tree. Another tree awaits those who continue north to Bly Gap. An iconic twisted oak tree invites hikers to sit on its knee and celebrate completing Georgia's portion of the trail. These icons are reminders and celebrants telling us to "Stay on the path!"

There were many physical challenges to come, but the trail was beginning to condition the body so that it no longer demanded full attention to hike this way. The stronger the body, the more room there was to shift my attention to the other parts of my soul. I began to explore why I was out here in the first place.

As the blisters of my feet healed and the soreness of my muscles subsided, the echoes of the years of bruises and scars to mind and spirit began to be heard in the solitude of the trail. This is what I needed; this is why I was here.

Beginning this journey in early March, I made it fifty-two miles to Unicoi Gap, near Helen, Georgia. There, my wife called to tell me that her sister was seriously sick and that her children were asking for help. So I stepped off the trail so that we could travel to Kansas and help. Family needs always come before other dreams. After a couple of weeks, I returned to the trail. Jumping up to the Nantahala Outdoor Center, there was an eighty-four-mile gap that would need to be completed later. The physical demand of climbing up from the NOC surprised me. I felt like my body had lost its strength to meet the demands of the trail. Once again, my body demanded my full attention on these ups and downs. My preparedness had strayed from the path during my time away from the trail. This was necessary but not enjoyable.

The sections ahead were stressful. A friend wanted to hike through the Smokies with me. David had joined me at the NOC, and we walked north together. I had not hiked with others very much. My brother and I had hiked a section of the Appalachian Trail as well as trails in New Mexico and Wyoming. We are very different hikers. Rick tends to focus on the miles, and I tend to focus on the views. He is much faster than I am, but I try to slow him down to see the beauties of creation. We complement one another well.

David and I had not hiked any distance together. Quickly, we realized that we had very different goals for the hike. David wanted to push through the trail quickly, and I felt the need to conserve my strength for the miles beyond this section. His rhythm was to hike late and sleep late. I enjoy early starts to enjoy the sunrise and to stop in the afternoon to rest and do the various chores needed to prepare for the next day. We were very different hikers, and this added to our stress. Rather than hiking our own hikes, we were anxiously trying to adapt to the other. We were both hiking "off the path," and it wasn't fun.

David returned home from Fontana Dam. I continued north. The first five miles into the Great Smoky Mountains National Park were the most demanding of my experience on the trail thus far. Those miles offered a grueling and relentless climb. Shuckstack Tower sits at the apex of that ascent and offers breathtaking views of the Smokies, but I could hardly enjoy the scene due to my exhaustion. I needed to find a way of getting back "on the path."

Each climb conditioned my body. I began to notice that each ascent became a little easier. My body was reclaiming its conditioning and gave room for attending to my mental side once again. Here another challenge kept derailing me and leading me off the path. Oh, I remained on the well-marked trail. As I have mentioned, the Appalachian Trail is well marked, and the GPS-driven Guthook app prevented me from losing my way from the physical route. But mentally and spiritually, I was not on the path.

We experienced all forms of weather. On Rocky Top Mountain in North Carolina, several hikers congregated and discussed the beauties of the mountains and valleys below where we stood. We talked about the heat of the day and the clear blue skies above. A few days later, I hiked for eleven miles in freezing rain from Clingmans Dome to Icewater Spring Shelter. We experienced heat and cold, sunshine and rain, and it was all good. The weather was unavoidable and really didn't bother me. The experience would be a source of great stories to tell back home. I embraced the weather, and this was the beginning of the trail's invitation for me to embrace all of the experiences that would unfold before me. This was the trail teaching me to "stay on the path."

Like many lessons, it takes a while for head knowledge to seep into my soul and become heart knowledge. The trail offered many opportunities for me to absorb its teachings. Each key landmark helped me to embrace the effort to reach it to enjoy its treasures. Clingmans Dome was my conscious beginning to really accept the value of staying on the path. As I walked upward to the highest point on the Appalachian Trail, I found myself in a mystical place surrounded by trees, standing and fallen, covered with emerald green moss. Although the sun was bright and its rays filtered through the branches of the spruce trees, clouds rolled across the trail and moistened everything. It looked like an enchanted forest where leprechauns might hide their golden treasures. The soulful rewards of these sights eclipsed the physical prices extracted to see them. This was the embodiment of the trail's lesson to "Stay on the path!"

I often forget this lesson when distractions arise, but the trail has a way of calling us back to its teachings. I needed to retake the examination over the next few days. Elsewhere I have shared about the crowded shelters that I encountered each night. After hiking all day by myself mostly, it was hard to express my emotional shock created by those evenings. The noise and crowds felt like a riptide pulling me out into the depths of ocean waters. I couldn't escape, and my soul gasped for air. The distractions dragged me off the path and disoriented me so much that I felt lost. Only by rising early before daybreak and getting back on the trail did I feel like I was back on solid ground. Still, my emotional legs were wobbly from the shock of the evening. Then I discovered Mount Cammerer.

I realize that I've described the evening that I stayed in the fire tower on top of Mount Cammerer. I don't think that I've expressed what that opportunity meant to me. Just as local trails had offered me a place of escape from the isolation I felt in the early days of the coronavirus pandemic, Mount Cammerer offered a place of escape from the overwhelming crowds encountered in the other shelter areas. Alone here, I took in the beauties of the mountains that stretched out before me and disappeared into the skies on the horizon. The valleys below were blooming into the greenest of greens that spring offers each year. Life was returning, and I was in the middle of it. The floor of the tower was mostly flat and level. I slept soundly on my air mattress and warmly in my sleeping bag. I brewed a cup of tea and watched the sunset. My soul sang a song of relief and peace.

That final night in the Smokies was as perfect as possible. The next day felt great. I had been given a view of what right looked like for me. Now the challenge was to discover how to hold onto the feeling and allow the lesson to sink deep into my heart. This was when I began to realize that I would need to hike a different way so that I could "stay on the path."

The shelter of the Mount Cammerer fire tower was a great gift to my spirit, as well as my body and mind. Here "stay on the path" held deep meaning. I was born into a family of faith. Our dependence on God was more than the social relationships of church. We often depended on God's care to give us "this day our daily bread." He never failed. My family trusted that he would keep us safe in dangerous military deployments and combat. Each of us came home with minimum physical injuries, though the emotional scars haunted us. They haunt us still. However, God's compassion leads to healing.

Following my military career, I listened to an urging felt deep in my soul to continue the path toward life's new chapter. He led me along a unique path of ministry. Even after seminary, I tried to stay true to what I felt was my calling. My time as a hospital chaplain was the most satisfying place where this path had taken me. I also felt pulled into seeking deeper communion with God. My heart was hearing a soft voice saying, "Just pull up a seat and sit with Me for a while." Oh, this wasn't some weird kind of experience where God wrote a message in the clouds. It was more of an intuition, an inexplicable knowing.

This bend in the path led me to a contemplative practice. I began visiting a Benedictine Monastery and witnessed the monks balance work and prayer. Here the emphasis shifted from doing, even doing for God, to simply being with God. It was special, and I wanted that peace. My life began to take on a rhythm, a rhythm of life that was very different than my career as a soldier.

After a while, I met Patrick, who was a fellow Anglican priest. Patrick and I began discussing my monastic experience. He told me of an Anglican Order of Saint Benedict. I reached out and was soon taking vows as a brother in the order. Benedictines pray. That's what we do. However, prayer is much more than sharing our concerns and desires with God. We do those things, but we are also quite within ourselves, praying as we walk a path into an intimate place where we simply be with God. That is the meaning of contemplation. I have discovered this is where my spirit finds firm footing. When my spirit is stable, my body and mind also find healing and wellness.

Somehow life had become busy. I had strayed from the daily practice of contemplative prayer. My soul bristled with the noise of the busy trail. Now, sitting on top of this mountain, I realized that my spirit needed to heed the lesson "Stay on the path."

When I planned to hike the Appalachian Trail, the books and videos warned of various things that could derail the hiker. Physical injury, mental breakdown, or financial burdens could all stop one's journey. Sometimes homesickness or employment opportunities would coax a person off the trail. However, no one mentioned family obligations. In fact, there are so many things that can force us to stop short of hiking from Georgia to Maine or Maine to Georgia that it is amazing that anyone completes the journey. Everything must line up nearly perfectly to enable someone to break from all the other demands and expectations of their lives for four to six months and focus on a solitary goal of completing this amazing dream. I admire those who do it, and I realize that they were both determined and fortunate. This is their path. In hiking phraseology, they are blessed to be able to "hike their own hike."

Sometimes to call to stay on the path means following the physical trail as it's marked and blazed. It is one way to listen to and learn from those who have traveled this way before me and learn from them. This lesson taught me to always embrace the trail just as it is and seek what it has to offer me. Staying on the path is a way of submitting to it rather than fighting with it. It is a way of accepting what the trail offers rather than trying to conquer it. The mountains, valleys, streams, creeks, roots, and rocks will always remain here as long as time remains. It is futile to fight with the trail, and these beauties are unconquerable. Rather than wasting my energy resisting, dreading, or complaining about the trails that face me, I hope that I will slow down enough to search for the joy that lies deep within this experience.

Sometimes to stay on the path means hiking a different way. During those final seven miles from Mount Cammerer to the northern terminus of the Great Smoky Mountains National Park at Pigeon River Bridge, I considered what it would mean for me to "stay on the path." The need to care for family and community back home ever increased its call. The trail had given me an opportunity for strength and healing. This had been a critical time self-care. For me to continue to thru-hike, I would have simply been demanding my way for selfishness' sake. Some needed to thru-hike, and the trail would continue to offer lessons to help them grow. I had other needs. I still needed opportunities to commune with creation and the Creator, but I could enjoy those opportunities by hiking sections of this trail as well as other trails less traveled. I continue to learn to stay on the path. Now it's time for me to listen to the trail for other lessons too. There are opportunities where I must step aside to see more.

CHAPTER 7
SOMETIMES YOU HAVE TO STEP ASIDE TO SEE MORE

"To step aside is human."

—Robert Burns

As I drone on and on about how important blazes are to hikers and I stress the need to stay on the path, you may get the idea that I never strike out on a new course, one that isn't marked or a destiny never explored. Kaat is a friend who listened to excerpts from my chapters about blazes and paths. She commented, "But sometimes you have to step aside to see more." Kaat is a fellow hiker who shares her adventures on the YouTube channel "Steps by Kaatje." I enjoy her wanderings, humor, and wisdom. She's right! Sometimes we do step aside to see more.

Stepping aside from well-worn paths and exploring uncharted ways opens new worlds; some are beautiful and rewarding; others are dangerous. Sometimes the beautiful and the dangerous share a common trail. Determining the difference, I believe, requires preparation and experience. The young man who sat on the top of Springer Mountain didn't seem to be prepared, and I don't think he had ever hiked before. Striking out to hike even well-traveled paths like the Appalachian Trail is treacherous for the ill-prepared.

As we plod through miles of trails on a variety of hikes, we gain experience to recognize dangers and to decide whether to avoid those dangers or try to manage the risk so that we can enjoy the rewards of exploring new things. Experience is a great gift. I like to describe wisdom as the product of education and experience. Education alone, whether formal education or research about a specific trail to hike, isn't enough. We probably know highly educated, well-informed people who are as dumb as the rocks we complain about as we hike the Appalachian Trail in Pennsylvania. Book smarts only prepare us for experience. I will use an old army term; "shave tail" refers to a newly minted second lieutenant. I can relate to this because I was one of those second lieutenants. The phrase comes from the horse cavalry days. Soldiers would shave the tail of a new mule to show that it was untrained and unreliable. They began to teach the mule how to carry its load and follow instructions. The schooling lasted until the mule's tail grew back, and then it was trustworthy because it had gained experience. We all begin as shave tails. We just may not be easily identified as rookies.

The trail is a wonderful teacher. We do well to listen and become good students. Education and experience produce wise hikers. I'll write more about Professor Trail later. I am beginning to recognize the lessons the trail offers. I wish that I was more attentive. I wish that I was a better student. I'm certainly not ready for extreme rock climbing or sleeping in a portaledge dangling off the side of a sheer rock face of a mountain. No, I have never studied how to walk along those paths, and I have no experience in doing it. Honestly, I have no desire either. Sleeping on sloping ground is bad enough for me. I cannot imagine daggling off the sheer rock face of a tall mountain and being able to sleep at all.

I have stepped aside to see more, and I've been blessed by doing so. When I shared my experience bushwhacking through the dense forest near the Dan River, I described the near disaster of discovering the cliff edge. Had I stepped through the ground cover and into space, the fall would have been bad. However, I knew enough to walk carefully and feel for potential dangers. Stepping aside held dangers, but there were also great treasures. The greatest treasure of that adventure was the fawn that lay curled up on a patch of smoothed grass. Her body was covered by the white dots of infancy. She was so peaceful, sleeping as her mother was out foraging for food. I stood back and looked, capturing the discovery with my camera and feeling as if I had discovered a pot of gold at the rainbow's end. Nothing could have been more exciting at that moment. I had stepped aside and seen much more than expected.

Other trails taught this lesson. There are many opportunities to step aside to see more. Four examples stand out from my walk through the Great Smoky Mountains. I am sure many trails to come will echo this wise maxim as well.

On the first official day of my Appalachian Trail journey, I began walking north from Springer Mountain. The weather and temperature felt like spring, but it was early March, and winter would make itself known soon enough, but not today. It was an exciting day, warm and sunny. As I walked, I first descended down into Three Forks Junction and then climbed up Hawk Mountain. After about five miles into the journey, I saw a blue blaze off to my left. There was a wood sign with "Long Creek Falls" carved into its face. I stood at the juncture. Looking ahead was the white blaze of the Appalachian Trail calling me onward. I planned to hike another three miles before stopping to pitch my tent, boil water for my instant dinner, and sleep my first night on the trail. But the blue blaze also spoke and said, "You may never come this way again. I have sights for you to see. Come here. Step aside and see more." I stepped aside and walked down the path toward the sound of rushing water.

At the end of the blue-blazed path was a waterfall. It was amazing! The trail had been sort of monotonous all along the way. Not monotonous in a bad way. It was all new and exciting. It is exciting to see the white blazes on the trees, the rhododendron that thickly borders each side of the worn pathway, and little log bridges that offer dry crossings over streams that crisscross the trail. These are common views as I walk. Then there are the openings between the trees near the mountaintops. Those openings are like nature's windows to show the beautiful vistas that extend from layer upon layer of mountain ranges, separated only by tree-covered valleys. However, here was something different. Here was more. Water cascaded down over rocky steps, foamed white by the power of its flow, and crashed ten feet into a pool where the water became crystal clear before rushing on down the creek through rapids around large boulders worn smooth by the ageless stream. Only a single overused word came into my mind as I stood there—beautiful! I was so glad that I had listened to the blue blaze, stepped aside, and seen much more.

Two weeks later, the trail once again invited me to step aside. I was tempted to ignore her call this time. I had entered the Great Smoky Mountain National Park. This part of the trail intimidated me. I felt like I was stepping into a wilderness where there was no escape. The only option once I entered was to go through. No turning back. I don't know where those thoughts came from. None of them were true. I discovered the same network of forest roads that intersect the trail from Georgia to Maine. Still, the Smokies seemed ominous. The opening climb that greets hikers from the little black box where we deposit our park permit and the next five miles is an unrelenting, grueling up. I met many fellow hikers along the way who rested and shared their personal doubts about making it through the Smokies, and we had just begun the journey. I continued to climb, clawing away at the core of my endurance and praying for this to be over.

Blood Mountain, Jacob's Ladder, even the 603 steps that ascended Amicalola Falls didn't compare to this climb. One step at a time, moving my failing legs and trying to fill my oxygen-deprived lungs, I finally came to the little stream that gave of herself to thirsty hikers who had made our way to her reward. Rose was a young lady who sat among the weary travelers filtering water from the stream. Rose was tired from the climb but excited to see all of the beauties of nature. She called out to me, saying, "Monk, you've got to go up the tower!" At the top of this mountain was a fire tower called "Shuckstack Tower." To get to the base of that tall structure that appeared to be made of an old-time erector set, I would have to climb another quarter mile over rocks and boulders. Perhaps this was a blue blaze to ignore. However, Rose kept telling me to go up and see the views. They were worth it, she said. It wasn't far, she said. It was an easy walk, she said.

I surrendered and began climbing toward the tower. My legs had stiffened from sitting too long. My lungs burned for air again. My body seemed to say, "Who do you think you are, and why are you doing this to me?" I shouted back down the side trail, "Rose, I hate you!" We both laughed. She was right about the views being worth the effort. They were great rewards. Of course, she wasn't as truthful about the distance and the ease of getting to the tower. Still, I knew even before climbing the tower that this was amazing. Each section of the climb offered a new revelation of beauty. When I climbed through the little hole in the floor at the very top, the views were wonderful. The sky was blue with white puffy clouds high above the mountains that extended out row upon row and disappeared beyond the horizon. It was as if the Smokies were introducing themselves to us, "Here we are, and you are welcome to visit. We aren't going anywhere and will teach you if you listen." I kept this view in mind throughout this part of the journey. The old mountains spoke truth. They were faithful, and they taught me about their beauty and myself.

As I entered the Smokies, they welcomed me with a grand, though demanding, "Hello!" As I prepared to leave them six days later, their farewell was equally spectacular. The next invitation to step aside was Mount Cammerer. A story of stepping aside to see more would be incomplete if I didn't share about Mount Cammerer once again.

Walking north on the trail from Tricorner Knob before sunrise, I enjoyed the now-familiar subtle changes in the sky and the birds cheerfully singing their welcome to me. It was a stark contrast from the night before, where scores of tents dotted the main trail before and after the path leading down to the shelter area. The serenity of the morning hike was very different than the chaos of the crowded hills and valleys that were filled with more tents surrounding the small shelter that was overflowing with hikers seeking refuge in it. In the solitude of the early morning, I felt a deep conviction that I would not repeat my nighttime experience again this evening. I began to plan for an eighteen-mile trek that would take me out of the Smokies. It was early, and there would be few hard climbs. I could do this. However, something inside gnawed at my emotions. I didn't want to leave this part of the trail just yet. I wanted one more night here, but I wanted to be able to soak it in and appreciate the experience.

These conflicting desires wrestled with one another as I searched for a compromise. My original plan was to hike from Tricorner Knob to Davenport Gap, a fifteen-mile stretch. There were two shelters within seven miles of one another. I thought the congestion of the hiker bubble might be diluted between these points, and others would hike through to Standing Bear Farm or beyond. Then a ridge runner stopped by as I ate lunch and told me that Cosby Knob Shelter was closed due to an aggressive bear that destroyed a hiker's tent. Without that shelter, Davenport Gap would likely be a repeat scene of last night's experience. I faced a dilemma. The ridge runner moved on, and I began looking at my narrow options. Suddenly, I looked at the Guthook app on my phone and saw a tower symbol. Perhaps there was another option. Perhaps I could step aside to see more.

After hiking eleven miles, I came to a blue blaze that marked the side trail to the Mount Cammerer fire observation structure.

It was another zero point seven miles to the building. The first half mile of the trail was smooth and mostly level. I met several day hikers who said the view from there was worth the visit. I didn't share my intentions of possibly spending the night there. Pushing on down the path, I came to a pile of boulders. The path disappeared here. It didn't veer right or left. So I decided to climb up the pile and see what I could see. The boulders kept ascending like a poorly planned staircase. Finally, I saw the white second story of the building. Windows, now mostly broken, surrounded the outer wall of the round structure. It had been built in 1939 by Civilian Conservation Corps workers. It must have been lovely in its day. It still was lovely, even if it was weathered with age, wind, and rain.

I really wasn't sure that Mount Cammerer would offer the retreat that I wanted before stepping through the propped doorway and listening to the strong breeze rushing through the broken windows and rustling the cloth material tacked over the openings. The old structure creaked and banged as the wind blew on top of the mountain. There were comments on Guthook by previous hikers who had stayed here. Some wrote about huge rats that visited in the night. Others commented that the visitors were not rats but friendly ferrets. Honestly, I didn't want either to disturb my sleep. As the sun began to set and the shadows descended on the panorama surrounding the tower, I knew this was the gift I needed for my final night in the Smokies. I was so thankful that I had stepped aside and seen so much more. Just as the Smoky Mountains had greeted me with welcome at Shuckstack Tower, they now wished me a fond farewell at Cammerer Tower. As the evening prayer says, "Lord, grant me a peaceful night and a perfect end."

My experience on the top of Mount Cammerer was healing for body, mind, and spirit. There was space to reflect and respond to the many lessons that I learned. I realized that I had been schooled by the Smokies and that my education was far from complete. There was a pause in my studies as I came off the trail once again to attend to other commitments, but my soul would yearn for the day when I could return to follow the blazed trails, stay on the path, and sometimes even step aside so that I might see more.

The next opportunity to step aside came when I returned to the section that I had missed from the Nantahala Outdoor Center to Unicoi Gap. After leaving Winding Stair Gap, I planned to hike twelve miles south to Betty Creek Gap and spend the night at a campsite. I was quickly engulfed by the flora and fauna of the trail. The skies were clear, and the sun was bright, but the green tunnel blocked much of the light, and the trail was cloaked in shadows. Soon two ladies approached as they walked northward, and I was walking southbound. They stopped to chat and said there was a small path ahead of me, and it was well worth the pause to check it out. After we wished one another "Happy trails" and parted our ways, I began to look for the side path. Soon, there was the junction. The white blaze showed the trail, but an unmarked but worn pathway led off to the left, beckoning the curious hiker to an unknown destination. I became that curious hiker and soon was very grateful to the ladies for their suggestion. Here the trees thinned and opened to a view across the valley and displayed more rows of mountains. The sky was blue; the air was clear and smelled of fresh forest scents. It was a familiar scene that was always new every time I saw it. I love these mountains and the gifts of life they hold within themselves. This is creation. Each opportunity to step aside is filled with the blessing of seeing more. The only thing that can prepare us for these gifts is the trail herself. She is the best teacher.

CHAPTER 8
THE TRAIL PREPARES US FOR HERSELF

"The choices we make in life leave behind a visible trail called character."

—Unknown

When the thought of hiking the Appalachian Trail began to stir in my heart, my mind began discouraging me from even attempting such a crazy thing. My heart said, "This is an adventure of a lifetime!" My mind responded, "You're too old to do it!" My heart said, "I'm in pretty good health, and I don't know what the future holds." My mind answered, "You have diabetes; your feet are going numb, and your back has given you chronic pain since you were injured in army parachute training." My heart said, "I need this to heal from the years of emotional cuts and bruises of life." My mind screamed, "You are not ready!" This conversation repeated itself as I walked. The trail seemed to interrupt my internal debate and said, "You're not ready, but I will train you all along the way. I will prepare you for myself."

The trail's classroom opened before I officially began walking on her well-worn lanes. It began as my brother (Rick), friend (Kevin), and I walked through the arched gateway and up the approach trail toward the natural water presentation of Amicalola Falls. After a short walk around parking lots and following the pretty stream that flowed by this path, we arrived at the base of the waterfall. There were the staircases that stood between us and the remainder of the approach trail to Springer Mountain. I trudged up more than 600 steps with thirty pounds of backpack strapped to my body. At about the midway point, my pack felt like it grew in size and weight. With every future mountain ascent, I would recall the feeling of air starvation while being drawn to indescribable beauty. Here was my first session of learning from the trail as she prepared me for my next lesson.

Beyond climbing the stairs at Amicalola and standing on the summit of Springer Mountain, I don't remember much of that first day. I felt appreciated as Rick and Kevin hiked with me. Their presence was a wonderful gift. I remember the unseasonably warm weather, blue skies, and bright sun. It was early March, but it felt like early May. The trail was slowly getting me ready for harsher and more challenging experiences.

There were many challenging climbs ahead. Often the descents were as challenging as the ascents. One ominous landmark was Blood Mountain. Its reputation was fierce. Standing at more than

4,400 feet, it claims to be the tallest mountain on Georgia's portion of the Appalachian Trail, and it's the first real hurdle for northbound hikers. The two-mile hike up the mountain was strenuous but not as challenging as I had anticipated. However, the descent was another story. Loose rocks, large rocks, slick rocks, and sheer rock faces greeted the wanderer with many opportunities to fall. I went slowly down these obstacles slipping and sliding all the way. It was dry and warm as I made this journey. Only a few weeks earlier, fellow hikers had completed this part of the trail in deep snow and ice. I was thankful they were safe and I didn't have to endure their experience.

Blood Mountain boosted my confidence. The trail had gifted me with a successful feeling. I had not conquered the old mountain. She continued to stand, her reputation intact, and would continue to intimidate future generations of hikers. She would gladly challenge me should I ever pass this way again. No, I didn't conquer; I persevered and learned from the trail's teachings. She prepared me for another lesson that she had in mind for a few days later.

My hiking buddy, Mike, and I had climbed up and down Blood Mountain, and we hiked the next several days together. After Neels Gap, we continued onward. The weather remained unseasonably warm and dry. However, we arrived at Low Gap as dark clouds began to fill the sky, and around two o'clock in the morning, those clouds emptied themselves onto the trail. The heavy rain fell to the rhythm of loud thunder and flashing lightning. After a couple of hours, I packed my gear inside the protection of my tent. Finally, braving the cold rain, I dropped the tent, rolled it into its little sack, strapped it to the top of my backpack, and started off down the trail. In the beginning, I walked along to the side of the trail, trying to avoid the streaming water that flowed toward me. Eventually, the trail taught me the futility of trying to walk on dry ground. There was no dry ground. I was now fording the Appalachian Stream, and the water rose to the bottom of my pants' legs. After surrendering to wet feet, I began to realize that I was not uncomfortable. My shoes and Darn Tough wool socks kept my feet reasonably warm. My fears of dying from hypothermia subsided, and I enjoyed trudging along in the rain. Another lesson taught and learned.

Mike caught up to me shortly before we reached the fifty-mile mark of the trail. He had mentioned looking forward to completing the first fifty miles. So I kept watching the Guthook app on my phone as we approached that milestone. Reaching the point, I took sticks and fashioned a large "50" on the side of the trail. Then I walked up a few feet, took off my pack, and rested as I waited for Mike. When he arrived and saw my homemade marker, we laughed together. I think that he was genuinely touched. It felt good to give this small victory to him. The trail continued to prepare us to appreciate simple joys. We didn't know that circumstances would soon separate us. At the time, we just enjoyed the experience.

Unicoi Gap marked the end of Mike and I hiking together. We had planned to stay at a hostel and resupply before getting back on the trail the next day. However, my wife contacted me to say that she was going to Kansas and help her sister. I asked if she wanted company, and we changed plans. The next day instead of returning to the trail, I joined my wife and drove west toward Kansas. Mike continued north from Unicoi Gap. It was a bittersweet lesson. Dreams are important, and family is even more so.

After visiting family, Connie and I drove back home and prepared for my return to the trail. My friend and creator of my video artwork, David, contacted me to see if we could hike together. To meet his vision of hiking to Fontana Dam and into the Smokies, I would need to jump up ninety miles north of where I had stepped off the trail. So David picked me up at my home, and we drove to Nantahala Outdoor Center in North Carolina. We got off to a late start, and lateness seemed to plague us for the next several days. After getting into our room at the NOC around midnight, my rhythm was thrown into a frenzy. The next morning, we started around ten o'clock, early for David but three hours late for my plans. We visited the outfitters to purchase permits to hike through the Great Smoky Mountains National Park and finally were ready to start hiking, or so I thought. When donning my backpack, one of the web straps broke. It was a rocky start. I went back into the outfitters to buy some webbing and a sewing kit. Finally, after some homemade repairs, we really were ready to step onto the trail and begin the long climb up from the NOC. The trail was teaching me a lesson in patience and flexibility. That little sewing kit proved its value, as I had to repair two more gear failures as well as give it to another hiker to repair their equipment. A hiking proverb is, "The trail provides." The maxim that I was learning was the trail prepares us for herself.

I was surprised that I had lost so much strength to hike during my short absence from the daily regimen of walking these ups and downs. It felt as if I was starting all over again. There were several factors that contributed to my atrophy. The most obvious thing was that I had not walked in these mountains for a couple of weeks. My body quickly lost its muscle memory for hiking. My feet and legs hurt; my back ached, and my lungs rebelled from what I was demanding of them. My rhythm was off. I noted earlier that David and I hike differently. Our body clocks were different, and our goals were different. I don't think either of us was comfortable.

Additionally, we began to encounter the infamous bubble that I have written about. The trail was becoming crowded, and I feared the congestion would only increase. It did.

On our first night out, David and I stayed at Sassafras Gap with several other hikers. There we met Rerun, Gourmet, and Brian (he had not been given a trail name). It was a cold night with the temperature dipping down to nineteen degrees. I was concerned for David. He told me that he had a thirty-degree sleeping bag and a liner that his daughter had sewn for him. Sleeping bags are rated by survival rate, meaning that the temperature is the lowest that one can expect to survive in severe weather. The comfort temperature is generally ten degrees more than the bag's rating. So David should be comfortable at forty degrees and risk hypothermia at thirty. I didn't know how his liner would add to the bag's warmth. I was cool in my seventeen-degree bag, and I wore a wool hat, leggings, shirt, jacket, and socks. I feared that I would discover a David popsicle when I checked his tent the next morning.

The sun began to rise, and so did I. With my gear rolled and packed, I boiled water for breakfast and washed up with a hiker's bath that consisted of warm water on a quick-dry towel to wipe my face and brush my teeth. It was about seven o'clock. I waited for a stirring from David to know that he was alive. All was still. The fellow trekkers rose to follow their own morning routines. We talked and laughed while David's tent was quiet and still. They soon donned their backpacks and departed northbound on the trail. No sound came from David. I was getting anxious. About three hours went by, and finally, I heard a zipper sound, and then David emerged. I was relieved and frustrated with myself. I should have checked on him. We didn't really know enough about one another to help each other in time of need.

The second night was warmer but not much. The temperature dropped to the mid-twenties. I was much more comfortable in my sleeping bag. I didn't worry about David. Again, we camped on an abandoned roadbed at Stecoah Gap. I decided the next morning to get up early and watch the sunrise. It was glorious and signaled a wonderful day ahead. I packed my gear and struck out. The challenge of the day was another infamous climb called Jacob's Ladder. This climb out of Stecoah Gap is only six tenths of a mile, but it climbs 600 feet up. There are no switchbacks, just straight up the mountain. It's breathtaking but not from the views. I wanted to tackle this challenge with no observers. So I left before anyone else stirred. I completed the climb in about an hour. Then I sat by the trail's side, ate breakfast, and was thankful this was done. The remainder of the day would be filled with the usual climbs and descents, but none compared to this first trial.

As I sat, the sounds of footsteps signaled that someone was approaching from the north. Boss walked up with his smile and backpack filled with four-foot-long timbers. Boss is a trail maintainer. He is one of the volunteers who clear the path from blown-down trees, fill eroded trenches with rocks and dirt, and sustain the trail for future generations of explorers. Boss stopped to visit. He shared stories of his own adventures, his love for the trail, and his admiration for hikers. I thanked him for his work and the dedication of all the volunteer maintainers that he represents. Soon he was off, walking down the path to tend to his section of the trail. She continues to teach me that one of her most important gifts is community.

Little did I know that Jacob's Ladder was preparing me for more challenging climbs. Two days later, I faced the five-mile grind from the entrance to the Smoky Mountains up to Shuckstack

Tower. I won't repeat myself about that climb other than to credit the trail for preparing me for that climb by first confronting me with Jacob's Ladder. The steady diet of climbing and descending two or three mountains daily conditioned my legs and lungs to accomplish more than I thought possible. There were more lessons offered by the trail.

I became physically stronger with each mountain climbed and each valley descended. The gaps, basically low spots between climbs, were challenging, whether going down or up. The trail prepared different muscles, joints, and vital organs by conditioning me for the next section. I felt as if the climbs far outnumbered the descents and wondered if I would eventually break through the atmosphere and climb into heaven's gate itself. After all, I had made it up to Jacob's Ladder.

As my body grew stronger from the trail's physical challenges, I realized that she was preparing me for something different. It was time for mental growth, and she was getting me ready to tackle another part of myself. Perhaps the most obvious mental challenge that I faced began at the apex of Shuckstack and grew exponentially and at every place I stopped for the night in the Smokies. The first night was Birch Spring Tent Site. Here was a collection of about thirty people who spread out in the area. There was a lovely stream that flowed through its middle and eased the chore of collecting water for cooking and the next day's journey. A few folks gathered in one corner and made a fire. Campfires are great places to gather, listen to others, and share your own stories. Some folks went about setting up their tents, inflating air mattresses, arranging their gear for easy access during the night, and easy re-packing on the following morning. Then there was the sound of little gas stoves lit to boil water for dinner. It was a pleasant vision of nightly routines. I quickly learned that even pleasant views could overwhelm me when the scene was overcrowded.

The paradox between the seclusion of walking alone throughout much of the day and the shock that I've tried to describe of entering the shelter areas in the evening was another lesson that I needed to learn. It taught me a lot about myself. I like people; I really do. However, constant contact drains me. I am a true introvert, gaining energy from being alone so that I can be healthy and engaging with people. This isn't an illness or a flaw; it's just one of many personalities that makes life interesting and fun.

Each day my body grew stronger, and each night, the emotional shock became more intense. In the first few days of hiking through the Smokies, I realized scores of hikers that shared the trail with me were growing. More and more people joined the adventure from Georgia. Some were slower than me, but most were faster. Old acquaintances were replaced by new faces. The personalities continued to shift, and the relationships were like rolling waves on the ocean. They rolled in, receded, and rolled in again. They were unrelenting. Most of these companions of the trail were great people. They were funny, kind, generous, and shared my love of nature. There were just so many of them. My main goal for hiking was introspection. I needed to get to know myself. That goal eluded me in this crowd.

The trail was underscoring my dilemma and hiding her answer until I was ready to listen and accept what she had to teach me. I climbed toward the observation tower at Clingmans Dome, and I began to hear her whisper, "I think that you are ready, but this will be a long lesson." The last few miles climbing Clingmans Dome were the most beautiful of all the beauties through the Smokies. As I walked toward the 6,612-foot peak of the Dome, the vegetation hinted of the greater elevation. The rhododendron gave way to spruce trees. The forest floor was covered with pine needles and bright green moss. The moss covered the trunks of trees and the sides of the trail's pathway. Clouds blew in and created a dense fog that would quickly vanish, and bright sun rays filtered through the trees until another cloud blew through, shrouding me again in its mist. All was quiet except for the occasional wind that whistled through the trees. It was mystical and beautiful. This was a different beauty than I had seen looking down into green valleys and across neighboring mountain ranges. I wasn't just looking at the beauty; I was experiencing it. I was in the middle of it. The experience softened me to begin to listen to others' advice. It was perfect timing.

Rick picked me up at the Clingmans Dome parking area. He drove from his home in Alabama to bring me the best trail magic of my journey. We drove into Cherokee, North Carolina, for food and a night in a local hotel. I washed my clothes and myself. We ate and talked. It was great! Rick asked a question that I mulled over in my mind for the next four nights in the Smokies. He asked, "Is it important to hike the AT in one year?" My knee-jerk was response was, "Of course, it is!" However, I began to ask myself if there was a better way for me to hike, and the Smokies prepared me for the answer.

Early the following morning, Rick drove me back to the trailhead, and I started north once again. The weather was cold and rainy. I layered for warmth and donned my rain gear to try and stay dry. After a few hours of rain, I always feel soaked. Today was no exception, and it was about forty-five degrees. I made it to Icewater Gap Shelter and was thrust back into the thick of the crowds. Here was where I really began to hear Rick's question, "Is it important to hike the AT in one year?" My answer softened to, "I'm not sure. What are the alternatives?" The following three days were wonderful. The weather had shifted again to reveal blue skies, perfect temperature for hiking, and the mountains seemed to reward us for successfully making it to this point of the Smokies. It was as if the silver lining had eclipsed the stormy clouds, and I knew that I would make the best decisions for myself to "hike my own hike," even though I didn't yet know what those decisions would be.

Each day I walked on a dry path; the sun was bright; the pines and spruce were green, and the views were spectacular. Charlies Bunion was a cluster of granite boulders that pushed their way up and out of the earth on the mountainside. This was another of the Appalachian Trail icons that hikers climb and sit on the top of these rocks to gaze at the world around them. On a clear day, the scene of row upon row of mountains stretches out before the onlookers and disappears as they melt into the horizon where the earth meets the sky. This was a very clear day, and the view was captivating. One guy sitting in the perfect spot called down to me, "I'll move so that you can see." His was a generous offer, but I said, "No, there are plenty of places to see. You should enjoy your view." Emotional health and self-care afford us the strength to be generous and compassionate to one another. We sat from our respective perches and drank in the view for a long time before I climbed down and moved on to see what lay ahead.

Each evening I lay in my tent, the floor sloping toward the left or right or downward toward the bottom side caused me to slide one way or the other throughout the night. The restless nights gave me the opportunity to build on Rick's question. Why was I out here? What did I expect to gain from this adventure? Was I getting what I needed from the experience? Were there other ways of hiking that might be better for me? Is it important for me to hike the AT in one year? These were the mental challenges that I dealt with, and like my physical fitness, I felt stronger to objectively deal with those questions. However, I needed to be alone to think. Even in the seclusion of my tent, I knew that I wasn't alone. If I wanted to talk out loud or scream at myself or sing to express my feelings, I felt inhibited by the crowd who would not appreciate any of those things. I was mentally ready to engage with the trail, but I needed to be alone with her.

My time with the Smokies was nearing an end. I knew that my final night was the final opportunity to hear her lesson on preparedness. She had prepared me physically and mentally for herself. The final opportunity for this lesson was the last night and the following day of hiking through these ancient mountains. She offered me Mount Cammerer, and I am so glad that I accepted the gift. This was the most intimate experience of the journey. I climbed boulders for about a quarter of a mile to reach the stone and wooden two-story structure that was the fire tower on top of this mountain. Inside the second story, wood rafters were designed in a circular pattern. Windows surrounded the exterior wall. Many of the windows were broken and covered with cloth or metal sheets that were partially nailed in place, but their corners flapped in the wind and banged against the window frame. The wind blew through the many openings and whirled around the inside of the building. The wood floor was warped in places, but there was plenty of level space to lay my air mattress and sleeping bag. I also set up the little backpack stove to boil water for my dinner and tea. I emptied my backpack and inventoried my gear. Everything was accounted for, and now I could enjoy the evening. It was a wonderful setting. The sky was blue; there were a few puffy white clouds were pushed along by the wind. The trees below were brown, with hints of spring green created by the fresh leaves that were beginning to pop from their buds. The trees stretched across the valleys and up the neighboring mountains. The mountains extended to the sky. The little fire observation structure was built with a walkway that surrounded the outside of the second story level and gave me a 360-degree panoramic view. The sunset was awesome. My mental lesson sipped into my spirit as I sat on the edge of the walkway, drinking in hot tea and the beauty of creation. I felt deep peace for the first time in my memory. There were no demands, no expectations, no interruptions, only me sitting in the midst of creation feeling the intimacy of the Creator.

The trail had prepared me for this moment, and I was ready to receive it. The word that comes to the front of my thoughts that describes this specific instance is "intimate." I've written before that the trail is a soulful experience. There are gifts for our body, mind, and spirit. Here on the top of Mount Cammerer, the gifts merged into one spectacular evening. It was an altering experience. The next morning was beautiful too. I woke before the sunrise and peered down from my perch. The valleys below were dotted with lights of homes and farmsteads, businesses and villages, which revealed the world was preparing for a new day. The sun began to change the colors of the sky. At first, there were subtle hues of pastel blues, purples, and pink. Then bright yellow and red rays shot up from the eastern horizon to announce, "Day is here!" It was glorious.

I repacked my gear, said farewell to my wonderful home of the night, and began climbing back down the boulders that led to the path that led to the trail. Feeling rested and lighter, I walked the final four miles to the northern terminus of the Great Smoky

Mountains National Park, where I deposited the second half of my permit and walked on. I reached the roadway marking two hundred and forty-one miles of trail completed. However, the distance was inconsequential, as I realized that not every adventure can be measured in miles.

CHAPTER 9
NOT EVERY ADVENTURE
IS MEASURED IN MILES

"Life is a journey that's measured not in miles or years but in experiences, and the route your life takes is built not of roads but of songs."

—Jimmy Buffett

Hikers can easily become consumed by the desire to knock out big miles. Some hikers shoot for goals of hiking long-distance trails in record-breaking times. That's fine; each hiker ought to pursue goals they set for themselves. Goals help motivate us to finish what we start. Without goals, we can quickly lose interest and stop short. That is one of the great things about the mantra "Hike your own hike." I don't tell anyone else what their goals should be, and ultimately, I must follow my own purposes for enduring the challenges of the trail for days, weeks, and months. The miles are less important to me than seeing new sites. Maybe that's one reason I like to video my journeys; I want to remember and share these experiences. That's one reason why I wrote this book. Not every adventure is measured in distance; some are measured by the heights the paths take you. Not every journey can be measured in miles; some of the most beautiful explorations are measured in elevations achieved.

I was introduced to this maxim about height-measured adventures during my first outing on the Appalachian Trail. It was that trip where I caught the hiking fever. My brother Rick and I hiked a section near Irwin, Tennessee. The ups and downs, which are now familiar, surprised me back then. It seemed that the climbs were endless. The trail went up the steepest sections in a serpentine pattern of switchbacks. This was like traveling on curvy roads. We walked back and forth but ever upward. I would see the sky peeking through the trees at the top of a section and breathe a sigh of relief, as I thought this would be the end of climbing, at least for a little while. To my surprise, the trail simply switched back and then continued up. It was a cruel joke. I could almost hear the trail laughing, but I didn't find the humor in it. Suddenly, I was standing on top of Big Bald, and I could see the views all around. The actual reward was discovered in the heights. The miles were just the price of the ticket to get there.

The trail continued to play that same trick over and over. It quickly stopped being funny. I'm not sure that I ever saw its humor. However, as I learned to embrace the trail for what it was, the joke was simply endured, like an old uncle who repeats the same tale at every family gathering. We learn to accept the annoying for the pleasure of the relationship. The rewards of seeing the streams, flowers, wildlife, and mountain heights make it all worth it. In fact, the rewards far exceed the price.

A few years ago, three brothers and I decided to go on a hike together. Rick and I had hiked together, but Roger and Mike had not hiked. We wanted to go someplace that none of us had seen. We decided to meet in Alabama, where Rick lived, and drive to New Mexico. There we planned to set up a basecamp and hike several trails from a central point. After a long drive across Texas, we arrived at the Gila Wilderness near a site where cliff dwellers had lived centuries before. Their dwellings were well preserved, and it was a fascinating place. Sort of a mix between desert, prairie, and tall mountains.

It was a couple of hours' drive to the nearest store. That store offered the only Wi-Fi connection for our phones and showers. The water was heated by local hot springs that offered an endless supply of hot water. The problem was to have enough cold water to keep from boiling us. The little store also had ice cream. We all love ice cream. A very kind and friendly couple operated the store. So we drove there a couple of times during our week-long excursion.

As we planned our various hiking routes, Roger commented that we should be able to hike about four miles in an hour. Rick and I looked at each other and grimaced. I don't remember if Rick or I replied that hiking is very different than walking on a track or sidewalk in town. Trails were more rugged, and heavy backpacks would slow us down. We hoped that the four of us could do two miles per hour. We discovered that too was ambitious.

Our first adventure began on our second day in the wilderness. It was an eye-opener. We packed a day's worth of food and gear and set off for a seventeen-mile loop. We waded through a river several times in knee-deep water, crossed a wide prairie where bears had been seen according to local rangers, then entered some of the lower mountains before circling back to our starting place. This first adventure ended the hiking experience for two of my brothers. Roger had gone about three miles before he called it quits. He announced that he was returning to basecamp. Rick and I were concerned that Roger might get lost on the way back or meet one of the bears that we hadn't seen. He insisted that he would be okay, so we relented and continued our way as Roger turned back.

Mike had continued forward as the other three of us talked. I didn't think much about it until Rick mentioned that Mike had kept the maps of our planned route. We thought that he might wait at the first junction so we could hike together. When we arrived at the intersection between two trails, Mike was nowhere in sight. Later he said that he had left candy pieces as a marker for us to follow. I think some critters probably enjoyed the sweets and may have laughed at us as we tried to decide which way to go from here. After a couple of wrong turns, we found the correct path and eventually caught up with Mike. He had twisted his knee on some of the loose rocks and was hobbling along in pain. We continued the climbs and descents of those mountains and eventually came to the paved road that went back to our campsite. Rick dropped his pack and walked the last couple of miles to get his truck and come back for us. I stayed with Mike, and we sat beside the road. It had been a good hike, but we lost two of our crew.

Rick and I planned to go on another trek the next day. It was an about-thirty-miles-round trip. We hoped to hike to a hot spring, camp for the night, and return the following day. As we walked through a gorge, the mountain walls stood on each side of the trail. The trail ran down a small stream of clear, cool water. A warning sign welcomed us into the gorge with a warning that flash floods were dangerous. I could see why as there was no escape from rising waters if storms struck. Looking straight up at the sliver of sky that was visible between the mountains, I prayed for good weather.

We walked for seven or eight miles before stopping for lunch. As we ate, Rick suggested that we find something that all of us could enjoy. I agreed. So we decided to return to basecamp and ask the others if they would like to strike camp and visit Mammoth Caverns. We were all glad to be back together. We were together, and that was the greatest joy. The trip was not about the miles but the companionship of brothers. Our only regret was that our brother Jim could not join us, and our brother Randy had died the year before. It was Randy's death that brought us close together. This was an adventure that can't be measured in miles. It was best measured by the heights of brotherly love.

The following year, Rick and I planned another hike out west. He wanted to hike in Wyoming, but it was getting a little late in the year, and winter comes early in the high western mountains. I asked some of my hiking friends for suggestions, and one mentioned that the Wind River Range of Wyoming was his favorite place. It soon became mine too. I spoke to a few others who had hiked in that area, watched a few videos, and suggested that Rick and I begin at the Big Sandy Trailhead and walk a circular loop that would take us east to Big Sandy Lake, north through Jackass and Texas Passes, west in front of the Cirque of the Towers, and south down the Continental Divide Trail to the trailhead where we had started. It was a four-day and three-night trip that covered about thirty miles. We both thought it would be an easy trip. We might get it done in three days. We were wrong.

The first section covered six miles with only a slight elevation gain. The trailhead sat at 9,113 feet, and the lake was only 603 feet higher. We had not planned for the windstorm that had blown through the area two weeks earlier. The storm had uprooted many trees, and rangers warned us that we should plan for a long first day of hiking. We encountered a few blowdowns, but it really wasn't bad. We had no idea what lay in wait a few days later.

Rick and I discussed the possibility of hiking on through Jackass Pass. We opted to tackle that hurdle on fresh legs the next day. It proved to be a wise choice. We pitched our tents off the trail on the east end of the lake. It was a lovely place. Prairie grass covered the rolling hills that surrounded us. Our tents sat on soft, flat ground. A couple of other campers were packing up from the night before. They had just hiked over for a one-night stay to see the canopy of stars that filled the clear sky. With no light pollution to contend with, the stars were as breathtaking as the mountains that lay ahead of us. Those hikers mentioned that a bear had visited the camp during the night. I looked around and found bear tracks. It had been a grizzly, and the tracks were impressive. I laid my hands side by side in the middle of the paw print and then moved my hands out to the edge of where they had been. The print was four hands wide. The claw marks were enormous. I prayed again that this huge animal had moved on.

We saw no more signs of bears that night. It was cool and beautiful. A full moon was the only competition for the stars that filled the sky. The view showed me how very small we are on this celestial home of ours, as well as how small earth is in the midst of the cosmos that swallows us. It is a humbling and inspiring sight. This was where I began to form the maxim, "Not every adventure can be measured in miles." Distance walked really didn't mean much. We had only walked six miles to this place, but the experience took me all the way back to my childhood of sleeping outside on our hill in the country and seeing the Milky Way cut its path through the stars, picking out the planets, and trying to identify the constellations while wondering how ancient astronomers could see scorpions and bulls in the star formations. They must have had great imaginations. This place sparked other memories of sleeping under other skies that were more threatening. The stars dimmed by smoke and explosions on the horizons. The smell of oil and gun powder and the steady sounds of artillery rather than thunder. This night was measured by much more than the miles that we walked to get here.

The next morning was clear and crisp, with temperatures around twenty-eight degrees. A light glaze of ice coated our tents. My puffy jacket and gloves felt good. I could see the mountains that we would ascend. They were beautiful and intimidating as they stood on the northern horizon. The lake sat still to the west, and spruce trees thickly bounded the southern and eastern views from our tents. After admiring the beauty and enjoying breakfast in the cool, fresh air, we packed and started on our way to the trail that would lead us up and over the two big climbs of the trip.

The first climb was through Jackass Pass. I had read this was the most challenging of the two passes. I didn't find it true. The elevation played with our breathing, but neither of us experienced any elevation sickness as we ascended from 9,719 feet up to 10,790 feet over a three-mile walk. We then walked down about 620 feet to Lonesome Lake before ascending again to 11,443 feet in one mile to go through Texas Pass. That 1,300-foot ascent was taxing but amazing. The wind whipped across the landscape on top of barren rocks. A wood sign understated the landmark. I felt like I was walking on the moon or some planet. To give you a picture of these heights, I can tell you Clingmans Dome sits 6,612 feet high and is the tallest point on the Appalachian Trail. We were walking up elevations that were nearly twice as tall as Clingmans.

After walking down the loose rocks and boulders on the northside of Texas Pass, we traveled in front of the Cirque of the Towers. This mountain formation is another of nature's beautiful gifts. Pictures are pretty but fail to convey the awesomeness of their grandeur. The Cirque is a formation of mountains that make a semicircle around a grand flat prairie. We walked four miles to our tent site. The mountains stood on the south, and a string of glacial lakes lay to the north. We had only walked about nine miles, but miles inadequately measured the day. No, some adventures are measured by the heights the paths take you. Some of the most beautiful explorations are measured in elevations achieved.

The Appalachian Trail held its own version of this maxim. Places like Amicalola Falls, Springer Mountain, and Blood Mountain demand a price to climb the miles necessary to see them, but they reward us with amazing views across the surrounding mountains as well as insights into ourselves as we stand before them and drink in the views. Perhaps views would be more appropriate than miles as a standard if we could find a way to measure them.

One such achievement was Preachers Rock in Georgia. I had been climbing a mountain for what felt like hours. Finally, I saw an opening from the trees and a huge flat rock lay prone on the mountainside. The sky was clear and blue. A few white, puffy clouds sat high and motionless in the atmosphere. I was alone. So I took off my pack, laid down my poles, took out a water bottle. Sitting and leaning against the backpack, I lost myself in the scene before me. The mountains stretched out layer upon layer, and the deep valley before me was covered with trees. Rivers, lakes, patches of farmland, and buildings were sprinkled among the trees. All of the effort to get here was worth it. Each time I find something like this, it seems like it is my first time to see it. Again, beauty seems so inadequate a word to describe it. While I lay here, searching for the motivation to move on to the shelter area where I had planned to stay, a ranger walked up, and we began to visit. She said that the shelter area was nearly full and I would probably take the final tent site. I groaned. Recognizing my disappointment, she suggested a stealth tent site that I would pass on the way to the shelter area. It was a small site with water but tucked back off of the path, and few people discovered it. I thanked her profusely and hurried on up the trail, once again motivated to find peace and quiet. Soon, I found the site just as she had described it. With my tent pitched and dinner prepared, I began collecting wood for a fire. It was a special night. Perhaps the miles traveled contributed to my rest, but I sleep peacefully with the view from the heights of Preachers Rock imprinted in my dreams.

A hiking friend talked about their rhythm of the trail. We all develop rhythms, and I like to hear how others plan their daily routines on long journeys. My friend said that he liked to fix his dinner at the last water source of the day before going into a tent site and preparing for the evening. Likewise, he packs up the next morning and hikes for an hour before eating breakfast. It is one way to keep food odors away and not attract unwanted guests during the night. I liked his plan and adapted it to my own ways. I enjoy waking early, before sunrise, and striking out on the trail. The predawn sounds of bird songs and rustling squirrels comfort my soul. The sun enchants the forest as its rays pierce the trees or rise up over neighboring mountains. I'm a morning person. Armed with my friend's suggestion, I began skipping breakfast in camp and finding a place further up the trail.

I often found an overlook to sit at and prepare my oatmeal and coffee. The Guthook app displayed little camera icons for scenic views. That aid helped me select my breakfast nook each day. Usually, there was a spot where the trees thinned, and a rocky ledge offered itself as a combination seat and countertop. Using my foam pad as a seat and pack as a chair back, I would sit my stove beside me and boil the water needed to rehydrate my gourmet breakfast of oats with a little box of raisins or some dehydrated apple slices. The coffee was hot but tasted like the tree bark that scattered around me. Still, it was the best view around. Fellow travelers began to notice my morning breakfasts. They commented how they knew I would be eating as they walked along the path. Sometimes they would accept my invitation to join me, but usually, they moved on toward their goal of miles for the day.

Two more examples of adventures measured in heights but not miles were not in the Smokies. They were discovered on the section that I had missed by getting off the trail for a couple of weeks. I returned to the Nantahala Outdoor Center to go south to Unicoi Gap. David and I had met there earlier to hike north, and I had continued through the Great Smoky Mountains National Park. Now I was alone and walking south. Both directions were demanding uphill climbs. I began this section in the early afternoon of that first day back on the trail. My destination was Wesser Bald, which was only six-and-a-half miles away and a 3,000-foot steady climb.

Before getting to the top of the Bald, I stopped by the Wesser Shelter. The familiar three-sided structure was surrounded by rock-bordered fire rings and sitting logs. There were no good tent sites, and I wasn't tempted to stay. I continued to walk and discovered a little spring where I filtered water for the evening. A family was hiking south, and we talked about the water and the shelter. They were from Florida, so the mountains were a great source of stirring conversation. I treasure solitude, but the sight of others is exciting, and the opportunity to visit is welcomed. After a good break, the trail called for me to keep climbing to the fire tower that stood at the peak of the mountain.

Arriving at Wesser Bald, I climbed the tower and looked at the familiar but new view of these ancient highlands. Another lovely gift. The weather forecast was for clear skies throughout the night. The moon was to be full, a blood moon, according to reports. I decided to do something that I had never tried before—I would cowboy camp. Cowboy camping is just lying under the open sky without pitching my tent. I laid down the fabric used as a footprint that normally protects the floor of my tent from rocks, thorns, and sharp sticks. The air mattress was next, and my sleeping bag was on top.

Several folks walked up to the top of Wesser Bald. They didn't intend to spend the night but only to enjoy the view. About twelve of us stood on top of the fire tower when one young man dropped to his knee and asked his girlfriend to marry him, and she said yes to his proposal. It was a sweet and unexpected moment to witness their engagement. I couldn't decide which reward was greater, the view or seeing young love flourish. Perhaps it wasn't an either/or but a both/and reward. Perhaps the combination of the proposal with a mountain vista background was greater together.

The next morning, I continued past Wesser Bald and toward Wayah Bald. Wayah Bald was very different. The fire tower on top of Wesser was built of steel and looked like a large spiderweb sticking up into the sky. The top was a flat wooden platform with no walls and an unobstructed view around the entire parameter. Wayah Bald also included a tower. That tower was a stone-walled structure with a roof. Clouds were beginning to fill the sky. I arrived early in the morning with hopes of seeing the sunrise. Just as the sun began to break through the dim eastern horizon, the clouds rolled in and diffused the view like smoke. It was still beautiful, but I witnessed a different beauty. As I began to prepare breakfast, the shelter of the tower protected me from the wind. Suddenly, the clouds ripped open, and briefly, the sun rays poured through with creation's light show on full display. I had walked the distance and climbed the mountain in the dark, and it was worth it. The heights were more memorable than the miles. The journey had become more than the accumulation of miles. It had revealed a beauty that could only be measured in heights attained. The trail continued to reveal herself to me as I learned to trust her.

CHAPTER 10
THE TRAIL REVEALS HERSELF

"I was no longer following a trail. I was learning to follow myself."

—Aspen Matis

There are times when I must trust the trail to reveal herself. Do you remember the part in *The Last Crusade* where Indiana Jones steps off the ledge and onto the camouflaged bridgeway that crosses a deep chasm? It's called the step of faith scene. I recalled that movie several times as Rick and I walked through the Wind River Range in Wyoming. Our hike wasn't as dramatic as the movies, but there were times when it was exciting enough. We walked there in bald, rocky heights where the only evidence of human traffic was an occasional rock cairn. There were no worn footpaths, no blazes, no people in sight, only tall snow-capped peaks above and brush-covered valleys below. I had not considered that we would hike a trail where there was no visible path. It was disorienting.

The army had trained me to navigate using landmarks and maps. We called it "dead-reckoning," which was a way of discovering where we were based on recognizable terrain, direction, and estimated distance. It had been many years since I had actually used those skills, and I was rusty. Technology has given us new ways of traveling, and I am thankful for GPS. I used my familiar Guthook app to plot our course for this hike. It was very useful, but there were times when GPS and the terrain just didn't match. Sometimes if we went the way that Guthook suggested, we would step off the edge of a sheer cliff. So we would back up and look at the terrain and little paper map. Old school. Those were the times that I was most unsure and learned that I needed to trust my instincts as well as the terrain as it revealed itself to me.

As we traveled up the rocky terrain, there were no paths worn from previous hikers. There were no blazes marking the trail. There were the occasional cairns that I have written about before, but we didn't know if these were marking an obscure trail or a staked-out hunting spot. Ahead were only more boulders, mountains, and the horizon. The only thing recognizable as sort of a path were gaps in the rocks that appeared as if they led forward. It is hard to describe. As we moved on, the path would just open up ahead of us. Like the "step of faith" scene that Harrison Ford made, the stone path simply appeared. We walked up and through Jackass Pass this way, the route reappearing each time as we neared the end of what we had seen before.

With our eyes trained and our faith strengthened, we trudged up Texas Pass. It was a challenging climb up some large boulders. Rocks were smooth and slick in places, and we carefully crawled up those natural slippery slides. I often referred to the Guthook app on my phone to see if we were even close to being on the trail. We usually were. As we descended from Texas Pass, the loose rocks and gravel created by ancient glaciers made our travel treacherous.

There were large flat boulders to walk over. I used my trekking poles to test each boulder before stepping on it. Some large rocks were unsteady on the gravel base, and when I poked them with my poles, the boulder would slide down the steep slope of the mountain. It was a ride that I didn't want to take with a large pack on my back. I poked one boulder that appeared secure, but my weight caused it to tip down as I stepped near its edge. My foot slipped off and was trapped between the rock and another one lying beside it. The large stone flipped back up to trap my foot. The thirty-pound backpack was like a magnet pulling me backward, and I fell. The fall could have easily broken my ankle, but Rick carefully helped me up, and the only injury was to my pride. The descent was long and steep. I was glad when we discovered flat ground and a visible path that marked our way across the prairie in front of the Cirque of the Towers toward an intersection with the Continental Divide Trail.

The path was easier to see on the Continental Divide Trail. More hikers had traveled this trail. We still didn't see any blazes, but the pathway was clear. Only junctions with other trails caused us to check on friendly technology to reassure ourselves that we were on the right course. Then we came to the place where a windstorm had blown down countless trees, which obscured the path. The devastation was amazing. Maintenance crews were working on cutting through the downed trees from the southern edge of the damage, but we found ourselves on the northern edge, and the trail was practically unpassable. Trees lay across the trail like a jumble of broken match sticks. They were piled up in fifteen- to twenty-foot-tall heaps and covered at least a half mile wide on either side of the path that was the Continental Divide Trail. I had seen war zones that were easier to negotiate than what lay before us. This was the scene for the next two miles.

In one place that was especially thick with fallen spruce trees, Rick and I decided to split up and search for a passageway through the obstacle. For a quarter of a mile, I removed my backpack and crawled under the brush, pushing my pack in front of me as I went. I had gone several yards when the fearful thought came into my mind, *What if the way ahead is blocked and I can't find a clearing?* I hadn't considered that we didn't know how far the damage extended. I don't know if Rick had similar thoughts.

We both came through the thick pile of trees. Each of us was a little scratched and bloody from the dangling limbs and brush. Rick had to crawl his way through as well. We were glad to be reunited and discover the area where maintenance crews had cleared the path. The remainder of our hike was a comfortable walk back to the trailhead where our adventure had begun.

There were other places where the trail was obscured by nature. My exploration of the Haw River near our home in North Carolina offered another experience. There is normally a well-marked trail along the banks of that river. I wanted to go out for the day to escape the drama of pandemic reports. The Haw River appeared to be an easy one-day hike. I planned to walk about seven miles in and then return to my car to come home. The path led from the trailhead near the small community of Rudd, along the bank of Lake Townsend, around an inlet, and ending at a road junction. The trail began with a descent followed a fairly level course before ascending sharply to the road. The return trip was almost a mirror of the same descent, level path, and ascent back to where my car waited for me. There was one thing that I had not considered. There had been several days of rain, which made its own impact on the area.

Parking at the trailhead, I stepped out of the car to the sound of rushing water. It was my first hint that the trail would be different for this day. Backpack strapped tightly and grasping a trekking pole in each hand, I stepped through the tree line that hid the river and saw what looked like angry, muddy rapids barreling downstream. Large trees stood out in the middle of the river. Some trees stood erect, others bent in the direction of the fast-moving current, and still, others had succumbed to the power of the flood and tumbled along the water path like huge match sticks. The power of nature is an awesome sight. The waters refused to be constrained by the riverbanks. They flowed out into the trees and over the trail.

Initially, I considered getting back in the car and driving home. Instead, I decided to find my own pathway and bushwhack alongside the flooded trail. I had not hiked here before, but it appeared to be a simple trail. Studying the topography of the map, I didn't see anything alarming or hazardous. There were no cliffs to fall from, nor water crossing that would be risky with the river beyond flood stage. The woods were fairly open, with no dense brush to hide dangers. It was still too cool for snakes to be out. So I looked for nature's pathway to lead me southward. On this outing, I frequently referenced my compass to be sure that I was walking south as I hoped. The trees were tall enough to obscure my view of the horizon, but I could hear the water to my right even when I couldn't see the river. The openings along the forest continued to reveal the way in short but continuous sections.

Soon I arrived at the inlet. The original trail would have been nearly one-half mile to the west, but where I found myself, there was a pile of brush on the water's edge. It wasn't just debris washed up from the flood; this was more deliberate. It looked like a tangled mess, but it was an assembled mess. Limbs and sticks were interlaced. Small trees had been dragged to the heap. I was examining the mound when there were two large splashes. Something had jumped in the water. I stood still and tried to remain quiet when a beaver began swimming slowly back and forth in the middle of the water. I had never seen a beaver in the wild, and this was exciting. He seemed as curious of me as I was of him. I decided to stop for some lunch, and he just swam a few feet away, staring at me. After my break, I walked north and retraced my path to the car. The trail had revealed herself and much more that day.

MacEntyre is another friend that I've hiked with on the Uwharrie Trail. He had told me about Birkhead Mountain, which is part of that trail, and I had hiked across that mountain earlier. He wanted to show me other parts of the wilderness that were less traveled. We began on the same path that I had seen in my first visit, but rather than staying on the well-worn path, we quickly stepped aside into tall grass, through a ravine, and up the side of an adjacent hill. We came to an opening and a wetland area. The bridge that had once crossed that space was gone, and we began to walk parallel to the marshy field that blocked our way. Once again, we walked down a short narrow path that appeared to end in the trees. As we neared the end of the path, it revealed another section of itself to us. Each time we would approach the end of the trail only to see her continue through the tree line. I thought of the old prayer, *Give us this day our daily bread.* We didn't see the entire way, but only what we needed as we needed it. The trail was teaching me another lesson in trust.

Once again, Rick and I hiked another trail. This was in the Appalachian Mountains, where we began at Clingmans Dome and traveled east toward Waterrock Knob. This is the first segment of the Mountains-to-Sea Trail, a 1,175-mile trail that traverses North Carolina from the Great Smoky Mountains to the Outer Banks. The first segment is nearly forty-seven miles of mixed trail that includes seven and a half miles of walking on the shoulder of the Blue Ridge Parkway. It has some of the most beautiful and challenging areas of the entire route.

After sharing its path briefly with the Appalachian Trail, the Mountains-to-Sea Trail veers to the east. Unlike the Appalachian Trail, this track is not well marked. There is a worn pathway, but side trails intersect, and I was confused. Especially when we were led off the Blueridge Parkway and up a mountainside to bypass one of the several tunnels cut through the mountains for vehicular traffic. Eventually, we would recognize a landmark and be again assured that we were on the path. This was an amazing journey where we walked along Deep Creek, the historic Mingus Mill, Oconaluftee Visitor Center, and up to Waterrock Knob. Waterrock Knob is the third highest point on this trail and stands at 6,293 feet. From its vantage, one can peer into four states on a clear day.

Oconaluftee was my favorite experience of our trip. We began walking before sunrise. Elk were scattered in a large grassy area beside the visitor center. A bull elk trumpeted his warning to the herd to announce our presence. None of these beautiful animals appeared particularly concerned. A few looked up from their grazing as we walked by it the dim light that proceeded twilight. The trail was not visible beyond the beam from our headlamps.

It was a different revelation of the trail. Each step lit up the path another step's worth. The light didn't provide much illumination, but it did offer enough to keep us moving forward. We entered a tree line that stood alongside Deep Creek. Suddenly, I came face to face with another bull elk. He was younger than the big guy who sang to us across the open field. This elk may have been kicked out of the herd by the older bull. He was eating grass among the trees and occasionally trumpeted his own song. The other bull answered as if to say, "You stay away from us." The young elk paid little attention to us as we walked by. I felt a little sorry for him. He must have been lonely. Perhaps the trail would eventually reveal a new life to him.

Sometimes the trail reveals more than just more trail. There are places where the trail seems to hide a special treat for the adventurer and then reveal a gift that it has been holding for the right time. It was my third day of hiking north on the Appalachian Trail. Starting the day from Gooch Mountain Shelter, I planned to cover eight miles to the next shelter at Lance Creek. I climbed over Ramrock Mountain through Woody Gap and a series of ups and downs as I approached Big Cedar Ledges. Views of streams, mountains, and valleys invited rest breaks all along the way. They were welcome distractions.

By late afternoon, I came to a section of the trail that looked as if a rockslide was blocking the path. The mountain wall on the left and the sheer drop on the right prevented me from going around the pile of boulders. Then I saw a blaze painted on the front of one of the huge square chunks of granite. This was just part of the trail, and I had to scramble up and over to continue on my way. Laughing at myself, I stored my trekking poles with the cords on my backpack and began finding handholds and footsteps in the rocks. Like a mountain goat, I climbed up about ten feet and over about thirty feet of stone path. The other side was not what I expected. I had anticipated a return to the worn dirt path bordered by tall pine trees. The trail had something different to offer. She gave one of her special gifts; it was Preachers Rock.

Preachers Rock is a large flat rock that lays on the eastern side of the trail near the top of Big Cedar Ledge. The rock is probably thirty feet by twenty feet and offers a flat surface to lay on and rest. The sun had warmed the rock, and it felt wonderful on this cool day with the wind blowing across the trail. The view was unobstructed at this height. The sky was clear, and I could look far out over the neighboring mountains, valleys, streams, lakes, and farms that were scattered across the way. What a present. The trail had revealed the unexpected, and I was grateful. She wasn't finished giving gifts to me that day.

As I lay on this perch, a park ranger walked by and admired the view with me. She then asked where I planned to stop for the day. I noticed the grimace on her face when I said, "Lance Creek." She had just passed that way and said that I would fill the last available spot there. Now I grimaced and asked for suggested alternatives. She told me of a small stealth site just up the trail where one or two tents could be set up. After she continued southbound, I reluctantly got up, donned my pack, and started north, praying that no one else discovered the secret spot where I hoped to spend the night. Soon, I located the marker the ranger had described and stepped through a line of brushes and into an open area that was an amazing site. Making a fire ring with rocks and gathering sticks from around the area, I pitched my tent and made a fire to relax and reflect on the day's experiences. The trail had revealed herself; I was grateful for her gifts; now, it was time to rest.

Regardless of the trail, terrain, or location, many of the lessons taught are the same. Some paths offer a different angle or perspective. Some emphasize one lesson or maybe a specific point of a specific lesson. Every journey teaches and blesses. Creation is so vast, and there is great wisdom embedded in her. These adventures have renewed my soul. They called, and I was fortunate to answer. They call still, and I hope to step onto trails less traveled so that I may experience more. I am now sixty-five years old. My health is good, though I can feel the effects of diabetes in the numbness of my feet. Neurotrophy is a scary experience. I fear the day may come when hiking may not be possible for me. So, until then, I want to see what I have yet to see. I want to hike where I have yet to hike. There are more lessons to learn, and the trails are great teachers. I know because I have been schooled by the Smokies.

EPILOGUE

"The trail is a great teacher. I pray that I become a better student."

—Wandering Monk

I recall the exciting feelings of deployments with the army. There were so many conflicting emotions that fed into that excitement. Fear of potential dangers, anger toward the disruption of my life, wonder of the discovery of sights unseen, and many more. The army had a great process following our return home from deployment. It was called the "after action review" or AAR. Our love for acronyms led us to abbreviate many things. Anyway, the AAR was a time to consider what we had done well, what we had done not so well, and how we could improve ourselves. This book has served as a sort of AAR for me. The trail has given all she could to teach me. Learning from her schooling is up to me. I think I've learned a lot. I know there is a lot more to learn. So I look forward to ancient paths that will be new trails to me.

The trails and experiences that unveiled each of the ten lessons that I have written about in this book are not listed in any particular order. They are written more in the way each feeds into the other and introduces the other. These lessons don't mean that life is filled with roses and beautiful sunrises. Sometimes the clouds roll in and block the sun's radiance. Sometimes the rain falls and chills the soul. Sometimes we leave the views from the mountaintop and walk down into the gaps where the world is darker, colder, and more demanding.

I learned that the descents were often as challenging as walking up tall mountains. The rocks and roots forced me to choose my footsteps carefully. The downs were treacherous. In all my hikes, I never fell while ascending a mountain. However, I fell several times while walking down. My foot would step on a wet rock. My toe would catch a root that was sticking out of the ground ever so slightly. The weight of my backpack would shift. I would be thrown off my balance and fall. It was a scary experience every time. I was never injured badly. Once my knee was sprained, and I had to come off the trail for a few days. I was often scratched and bruised. My pride was always the most injured by every fall. That was probably a good lesson. However, I knew that the downs and falls were simply part of the hiking experience. They didn't define it. There were downs, but for every down, there was an up. I would get up again, walk up again, reach the top of another mountain, and there see again the wonders of creation stretching out in front of me like a sea filled with waves of peaks and valleys. The beauty was in the relief. All mountaintops would look like a boring shelf. All valleys would look like a sinkhole. Beauty was discovered in the mix of ups and downs. I may want to avoid the pains and hurts of life, but they offer me a contrast to the happy hills of being alive. My joy isn't a captive of my happiness. It isn't threatened by my pain. As I embraced the trail's ups and downs, I learned that joy transcends both. Here is a gift the Creator has given to me through creation. For every down, there is an up.

Still, the trail doesn't demand that we endure pain unnecessarily. Often, pain offers a path to healing. My unused, undeveloped muscles ache when they are subjected to miles of climbing and descending mountains, wading through streams, or walking over sharp rocks and exposed roots that crisscross the path stretching out in front of me. After a few days and a few doses of "vitamin I," as hikers refer to ibuprofen, my muscles grow stronger, and the hurt begins to fade away. If pain persists, then it should be checked; something more serious may be shouting for attention. I learned this lesson through the pain of a shoulder strap that dug into my chest. The trail also taught it to me when I hurriedly laced my shoes before a long day's hike. The constant rubbing of the sole of my foot against the sole of my shoe gave me a huge blister. If something doesn't feel right, check it! That was what I learned from these experiences. It's a lesson that I continue to hear as I check my gear and myself before striking out on other adventures.

We don't walk on any trail very long until we discover a tree that has been tipped over by the forces of nature. Rain falls, and wind blows. Large trees that appear to reach ever heavenward succumb to the powers acting against them, and they topple. The contrast between a tree standing proudly in the forest and a tree blown down, lying on its side, always amazes me. The clash of powers. As I began to look more closely at the blown-down trees, a common weakness became evident—their roots! The trees were blown over, and the roots lifted the soil where they were once embedded. Now a large cavity remained where the tree roots drew their sustenance. The roots were twisted and jumbled like a knotted string. They spread wide, but not when compared to the height of the tree; the roots were not deep. Broad, shallow roots had failed to anchor the tree during the storm. A great lesson learned about life itself. Deep roots of family, values, and faith secure me from life's inevitable tempests.

I was taught to follow the blaze when I began to venture out on longer trails. Following the blaze has its own learning points. It is a lesson in faith and trust as well as humility and obedience. Faith is so much more than simply believing something or someone. Faith is meaty; it has substance to it. It demands action. If I have faith that the blaze is leading me in the right direction, then I step out on the trail and walk. I am excited when I see the next blaze, and I trust that it is carrying me forward to where I want to go. Faith goes much deeper than the design painted on the tree or rock. The lays in what the blaze represents. It represents the one who painted the symbol and the one who blazed the trail in the first place. On the surface, I followed the blaze and felt comforted by its presence. In reality, I followed the ones who had gone before and took the time to show me the way. The deeper my faith became, the more I considered the blazers. I was humbled to think that they cared enough for so many they would never meet that they endured these hard ups and downs first and marked the way for us. My obedience to follow those blazes was not because they lorded some authority over me. No, I obediently followed because I recognized they cared enough to teach me.

As I began to consider taking up hiking as a serious pursuit, I thought of several examples of celebrity hikers that I enjoy following. I have watched hours of videos by Darwin on the Trail, Follow Bigfoot, and Dixie's channel called "Homemade

Wanderlust." These wanderers inspired me to get out there and walk. They continue to hike long trails like the Appalachian, Continental Divide, and Pacific Crest Trails. I dreamed of big hikes, long hikes, and challenging hikes. However, I discovered that short hikes were rewarding too. Whether walking eight to fifteen miles on a trail near home, a three-day hike in the Uwharrie Wilderness, or a longer two-hundred-mile hike on the Appalachian Trail, each outing offered adventures of a lifetime. There were views to be seen that would never again be possible. Geese, herons, sleeping fawns, and swimming beavers were all discovered during short outings. Likewise, my life goals may be so focused on the big accomplishment that I may overlook the laugh of a child, the caress of a loved one, or the sunrise that reminds me that I am fully alive and blessed. Creation is huge, but sometimes the Creator reveals Himself in the smallest of things. Sometimes He whispers to me in a gentle breeze. No, bigger is not always better. Often, the best is what we stop and notice, like a snail, a beetle, or a butterfly that seems to escort me up the trail as I walk along the path.

Early in my hiking experience, the trail taught me to "Stay on the path." It soon became my farewell in each video that I released. However, I didn't fully understand its meaning until much later when David and I discussed it as we hiked together. Good friends help draw out unseen meanings of many things. I may not yet understand the full meaning of "Stay on the path," but I do understand it more fully than I did when it was first revealed several years ago. Life often attempts to lure us off the path and detracts us from fulfilling that thing for which we were created. I have veered off course only to discover the less satisfying. While some of the blue blazes of life were exciting for a while, they didn't satisfy my deep longings. Some were useful, others destructive. The trail taught me the one thing that is constant is the trail herself. Whether I hike or not, the trail is there, and she is waiting for me when I return to her. It takes a lot of trust and faith to follow the way that others have followed and successfully finish the journey that I hoped to complete. This is what it means to "stay on the path."

Following blazes and staying on the path teaches the wanderer to recognize potential dangers and teaches us to work through the inevitable risks associated with entering all of nature's elements, the beauties and the threats. I mature as I walk in others' footprints. As I gain wisdom of the trail, I can expand my horizons to see more. Sometimes I must step aside to see more. There are views and wonders to experience beyond the well-worn paths. We are created with an adventurous soul. When I consider the explorers of the past and present, even the first person to adventure on this trail that is now followed by many, I realize there was no trail when that person walked this way. Stepping aside to see more is the call of those who have been filled to the brim by their experiences and realize there is more to be seen. Realizing and assessing the risks, I am willing to take the chance. I must be willing to embrace the results. Stepping aside, I see more. What I see more of is the alluring unknown.

Like many others, I was concerned if my body was ready to endure the daily regimen of walking mile upon mile with a heavy pack filled with all the gear to sustain me on the trail. I am generally in good health, especially for a sixty-five-year-old man whose body has been pounded about by years of army service. I was diagnosed with diabetes a few years back. My mother was severely diabetic and eventually died from the effects on her heart. I call it her gift to us, "the gift that keeps on giving." I have five brothers. Of the six of us, five have contracted this frustrating disease. However, hiking has blessed me. Walking these trails resulted in controlling my diabetes to the point that my doctor took me off all its associated medication. Oh, I still take pills for hypertension and cholesterol. I still take a baby aspirin as a preventive. But health is good overall. However, long-distance hikes are demanding. Make no mistake about that, and I questioned my ability to endure.

The lesson "The trail prepares us for herself" was personally important. I watched videos where others spoke about their fitness routines to prepare for a big hike. I spoke with my brother Rick who is the culprit who got me hooked on hiking. I read books and listened to podcasts. The common takeaway from all this research was that the best way to prepare for the hike is to hike. As I stepped onto the Appalachian Trail, the wisdom of that advice became clear.

Our culture often prays like this, "Lord, grant me patience. And give it to me right now!" We want instant success and instant gratification. The trail will quickly humble students who are willing to learn a different lesson. I watched hikers who were physically toned and strong, who thought they could conquer any challenge the trail could offer. I watched young men and women who bragged about their invincibility. I saw them push too hard, too quickly, and injure themselves. The trail blazers in Georgia were brilliant. They constructed shelters at eight-mile intervals. They seemed to know that beginners should pace themselves. An eight-mile day was a good day. It was a great day. It was enough to listen to the trail as it prepared us for the next lesson. The Georgia portion of the Appalachian Trail is filled with ups and downs, rocks, boulders, mud, water crossings, and all of the other things that will be discovered as hikers move up the next 2,115 miles to

Mount Katahdin in Maine. Georgia is a sort of box of assorted chocolates, a sampler of all the other parts. It is the AT-101 course in the grand lesson "The trail prepares us for herself."

Hiking connects me to nature. I see the big and the small, the beauty and the not-so-beautiful. However, it is so much more than just seeing nature. Hiking immerses me into nature, causing me to realize that I am part of it. I don't stand above it, but I have a role to play like every other part of it. Hiking helps me contemplate my relationship with the rest of creation and get back to the simplicity of communion with creation and the Creator. I have discovered that trudging through the mountains and gaps is much more than just walking miles. If miles become my destiny, then I lose the pearl of great price that the trail holds out as my reward.

Some trails that I have walked refuse to be measured in miles. Oh, there is distance from the starting point to waypoints. There are miles from the beginning to the end, but the trail measures herself with a different measure. In the Wind River Range, the miles from Point A to Point B failed to depict the price demanded to ascend Texas Pass. It was only a one-mile climb, but the heights achieved over that mile were far beyond measure. The experience was glorious. The air smelled crisp and fresh; the sky was the bluest of blues; the surrounding mountains demonstrated the strength of God's hand. To talk of miles on this path was to cheapen the grandeur of this place. Some adventures cannot be measured in miles, but they are measured by the heights they take us.

The trail taught me to look beyond, look beyond my limitations, preconceived ideas, prejudices, and ego. No matter what I feel or believe, reality is bigger than me. When I open my eyes with the desire to see the yet to be seen and ears to hear the yet to be heard, I discover a treasure waiting for me. The voice inside me says, "This is what is real. Listen to me, and I'll teach you more than the failed philosophies of the world." It's true too. I find the simple things like a flower, beetle, butterfly, deer, and bears seem satisfied being what they were created to be. I begin to embrace that same satisfaction of being what I was created to be. That is the definition of glory!

If you want to learn any of these lessons, there is a single maxim tying all others together. This teaching holds the secret to embracing the schoolhouse of the Smokies. It is a lesson of trust. I must trust if I am to see. The Bible describes faith as "…the substance of things hoped for [and] the evidence of things not seen" (Hebrews 11:1, KJV). Faith is much more than belief. I may believe something, but without trust, then I will refuse to experience it. Faith is substance. It has weight to it. It is filled with power. Faith pushes me forward toward the unseen. Faith demands trust. Sometimes the trails were not visible. In Wyoming, the way forward was up and through boulders that refused to show the worn path that others had walked. Instead, the trail would show herself through passes and around openings. Even on the Appalachian Trail, there are places where the familiar worn pathway disappears in rocky crags that demand hikers scramble over boulders. The trail then reveals herself to trained eyes educated by the trail herself. These are the classrooms of faith-building. These are the places where creation reveals itself, and if I look close enough, I see the fingerprints of the Creator.

The final lesson learned in this book will not be the last lesson that I learn. At least, I hope it isn't the last. I know the trail has much more to offer, and I want to be a good student. The trail continues to reveal herself on every step of every journey. I continue to hear her calling for me to "Stay on the path."

ABOUT THE AUTHOR

Wandering Monk went to find himself by hiking through the Smoky Mountains on the Appalachian Trail. Dan Nobles describes himself as boring, but after three tours as an army colonel in the Pentagon and becoming an abbot in the Anglican Benedictine Order, it's hard to think of him as boring.

Dan's education includes a BS degree in engineering technology, one MS degree in international relations, and another in advanced strategic arts, plus a doctorate in theology. He has served as a military commander, a hospital chaplain, strategic consultant, senior administrator in private schools, mentor to youth, and ordained minister of gospel and church. He is well-acquainted with earthly life and death situations as well as those of eternal consequence.

He began hiking to find his own healing and respite for his soul—wounds and battle scars can run deep in the physical, emotional, and very much so in the spiritual. They can occur at times when you don't have the time to process through and deal with them all. Dan decided to deal with them all, each as they come to the surface in the solitude of the hike, in the beauty of creation, in his determination to keep putting one foot in front of the other, and in learning the lessons the trail will teach you—like take extra care when you step where you can't see.

Dan is the youngest of six brothers who grew up in the rural South. From his parents, he learned to do an honest day's work for an honest day's wage, leave things better than you found them, and clean up after yourself. From the military, he learned how to keep his head, how to make tough decisions, and how to keep going when the going gets tough. From the Lord, he learned he has a lot more to learn, starting with acceptance, forgiveness, and restoration. Well, what else might you expect from a monk?